D1601586

BEHOLD, IT IS I

Behold, It Is I

Scripture, Tradition, and Science on the Real Presence

STACY TRASANCOS, PHD

FR. GEORGE ELLIOTT

TAN Books
Gastonia, North Carolina

Cover design by Caroline Green

Cover image: Holy Eucharist, photo by Prachaya Roekdeethaweesab/Shutterstock

Library of Congress Control Number: 2021941499
ISBN: 978-1-5051-1724-0
Kindle ISBN: 978-1-5051-1725-7
ePUB ISBN: 978-1-5051-1726-4

Published in the United States by
TAN Books
PO Box 269
Gastonia, NC 28053
www.TANBooks.com

To Annie Paniagua

Blessed Carlo Acutis, pray for us.

On the night of that Last Supper,
seated with His chosen band,
He the Pascal victim eating,
first fulfills the Law's command;
then as Food to His Apostles
gives Himself with His own hand.

Word-made-Flesh, the bread of nature
by His word to Flesh He turns;
wine into His Blood He changes;-
what though sense no change discerns?
Only be the heart in earnest,
faith her lesson quickly learns.

Down in adoration falling,
Lo! the sacred Host we hail;
Lo! o'er ancient forms departing,
newer rites of grace prevail;
faith for all defects supplying,
where the feeble sense fail.[1]

—St. Thomas Aquinas

1   St. Thomas Aquinas, "Pange Lingua Sing, My Tongue," https://www
.preces-latinae.org/thesaurus/Hymni/Pange.html.

CONTENTS

FOREWORD

I am pleased to offer some brief comments regarding the book *Behold, It Is I*, which Father George Elliott and Doctor Stacy Trasancos have collaboratively offered to all who believe in the Real Presence. An initial thought is that the title is exactly expressive of the reality they explore. Many of us lament that we live in times where too many in the Catholic Church express ambiguity and even outright disbelief regarding the Eucharist. In this context, the title these good authors have chosen gets to the heart of the matter. The title, *Behold, It is I*, offers a Person speaking in the first person. As one man who has been blessed to continue to grow in his Eucharistic faith, I can say that much of that growth comes down to a deeper understanding that from the altar or from the tabernacle, an actual Person speaks to us. We all need to rekindle this kind of faith in our own hearts. This faith transformed the lives of the saints of old and gave many of them the strength to die rather than to deny their Eucharistic Lord. This is the kind of faith that I believe this book can nurture for those who take the time to read it. We must move from an abstract approach to the Eucharistic presence of the Lord to a more concrete and realistic approach. I believe this book can help us to focus more deeply on our faith, which says that the consecrated bread and wine that have become the body and blood of Jesus Christ are not an abstract idea. The Eucharistic presence of our savior and Lord is the opposite of abstract; He is really, concretely, and dynamically with us. Let us hope the reader will grow in a deeper encounter with Jesus Christ who promised that He is "with us until the end of the age." May this faith resonate through the Church and strengthen us in Him.

Turning to the subtitle of this book, *Scripture, Tradition, and Science on the Real Presence*, the authors have once again given the reader an important focus. As we embrace the truth proclaimed by the Catholic Church that the Eucharist is the "source and summit" of our Faith, this subtitle encompasses the entirety of this faith. One of the great strengths and blessings of the Church through the ages is the reality that we embrace both Scripture and Tradition. This highlights the important reality that in many ways the Church is a "both and" community. Since the beginning of Christianity, there has been a tendency to focus on one or the other and abandon "both and." This is most dramatically significant in the person of Jesus Christ Himself. The early Church saw centuries of struggle with the question that Jesus raised as He walked this earth. One can say that Jesus of Nazareth was ultimately crucified because He claimed to be both God and man. Certainly, even for His disciples who believed Him to be truly the Son of God, the clarity of how this could be as expressed in the technical language of the hypostatic union would take centuries to develop. Even now we must admit that how Jesus Christ can be fully God and fully man is beyond our understanding.

Our struggles with coming to a deeper understanding of Jesus of Nazareth is naturally highlighted in our struggles to understand the Eucharistic presence He has left us. We look to Scripture and Tradition to understand the

God-Man, Jesus Christ, and we look to Scripture and Tradition to understand His Real Presence with us in the Most Blessed Sacrament, the Holy Eucharist. The great mystery that Jesus is the Incarnate Word can only be more deeply developed when we understand that Sacred Scripture is Jesus Christ. Through the two thousand years of Tradition, the faithful have constantly turned to Jesus present in the written word in order to more fully understand Him present in His incarnation and in His Eucharistic presence, which mysteriously continues His incarnate presence in the world.

Finally, turning to the additional term in the subtitle, *science*, I believe this volume broadens the focus of the reader in a significant way for this twenty-first century. We live in a time when for many, possibly most of humanity, science has become god. As we contemplate the beautiful meaning of the Blessed Sacrament and its essential role in the life of the Church, it is important that science be brought into the discussion. In a way, science is the third element that must be addressed, along with Scripture and Tradition, in our age. We must honestly bring our questions and our uncertainties to Jesus in Scripture and then to Jesus in Tradition, who then moves us in our day to address Jesus in science. And yet, this book will leave those who embrace science as their religion disappointed because their questions will not be answered in scientific terms. On the contrary, I pray this book will take believers into even deeper realms of mystery—mystery that is informed by reason and analysis but ultimately remains mystery.

Those who know their Lord and Savior present in the tabernacle and on the Eucharistic altar will find their faith nurtured and expanded as they read this book. And may

their deepened faith inspire them to engage our too often
faithless world with the joy and the hope that is Jesus Christ.

+MOST REVEREND JOSEPH E. STRICKLAND
Bishop of Tyler

ACKNOWLEDGMENTS

W E express many thanks to the people who helped us develop the ideas and texts of *Behold, It Is I*, including Hope Zubek, Kyle Sherling, Father Joshua Neu, Father Justin Braun, George and Andrea Elliott, and Maria Edens.

We are especially grateful to Dr. Oscar Paniagua, his wife, Kristina, and their family. One Sunday after Mass, Kristina asked their daughter, Annie, to research the Real Presence of Christ in the Eucharist. During the Eucharistic prayer, Annie had been inattentive, as is so natural for children. Annie discovered a video about Eucharistic miracles in Buenos Aires and sent it to her parents. They sent the video to Bishop Joseph Strickland, and he sent it to Stacy Trasancos, urging the executive director of his St. Philip Institute to research the topic and consider giving a presentation to the people of the Diocese of Tyler. Those talks led Father George Elliott and Stacy to the idea of writing this book. It all started with the excitement of a child. Kristina later remarked, "It's a good reminder to me that the little things have the potential to make a big impact."

INTRODUCTION

THE LOGIC OF BEHOLD, IT IS I

On Faith

THIS is a book about faith. When dealing with apologetic proofs, the theological virtue of faith can seem unnecessary. Some may argue that a proof should stand on its own legs top to bottom, that every logical step can be demonstrated and obvious. But this is not how proofs work. They always begin with starting assumptions.

Doctrinal proofs begin with belief in the testimony, or the revelation, of Jesus Christ. It is not possible to grasp the mysteries of the divine without the gift of faith. As St. Thomas Aquinas points out in the *Summa Theologiae*, "the reasons that are brought forth by the Saints to prove the truths of the faith are not demonstrative, but persuasions or manifestations that what faith proposes is not impossible" (II-II, 1, ad. 2).

In other words, the task of Catholic apologetics is to prove that what the Church teaches is reasonable and to delineate a logical path from Divine Revelation, which we grant intellectual assent to as an act of theological faith, forward to derive dogmas and doctrines. Apologetic proofs disprove a given mystery's *impossibility*. Scientific proofs, likewise, begin with observation (instead of revelation),

1

and equalities, formulas, laws, and theories are derived from there.

Here, in one work, we provide the most convincing proofs for the Real Presence of Christ in the Eucharist from Scripture and Tradition, notably the Fathers of the Church. Additionally, in keeping with modern times, we meticulously examine the scientific data from three of the approved investigations of Eucharistic miracles in the Church. This book will not, however, convey the message that Eucharistic miracles *prove* the Real Presence of Christ in the same way that Scripture and Tradition do.

Each proof deals with its own starting assumptions, especially in the case of science, with its limitations. In faith, we believe and profess that Jesus Christ is really and truly present in the Eucharist. We believe this in faith because we accept the testimony of Christ Himself. With each of these proofs, the reader will have to make an act of faith, either in God, which is most reasonable, or in another human being, which is far less certain.

We hope that the scriptural section of this work will sway any reader who believes God's Word is spoken through the Scriptures. We are confident that the Fathers of the Church will convince anyone who trusts the early Christian writers and the Holy Spirit working through them. Finally, we pray that the study of Eucharistic miracles, specifically the scientific findings and historical accounts, will strike the reader with greater appreciation. More than anything, we must warn you that detailed scientific investigations on their own will leave you wanting. The human limitations of the scientific method will ultimately point you in humility right back to the simple words of Christ, "This *is* my body."

More than humility, the theological virtue of faith requires the life of grace. Well accustomed to the disciples' dilemma in Matthew 13:11, we know that those who believe do so because "to [them] it has been given to know the secrets of the kingdom of heaven." Therefore, we ardently pray and trust that our Lord will lavish you, the reader, with the grace to make an assent of faith and to accept fully the gift of the Real Presence of Christ in the Eucharist.

On Certainty

A fundamental framework required to approach apologetics is an understanding of the types of certainty. Apologetics is essentially the art of explaining why one has sufficient certainty to believe what one believes and the art of convincing the other to consider one's beliefs sufficiently certain to accept them.

Apologetics would be simple if we could have absolute certainty beyond any possible doubt in matters of faith, such as if Jesus Christ sat down next to us and offered up His Body. He did do that, and even then, people doubted! But that is the thing about faith: "faith comes from what is heard" (Rom 10:17), and what is heard leaves some room for doubt in an unbeliever. Therefore, in apologetics, we deal with degrees of certainty and accept that there is always the possibility that the other person will have doubt.

The distinction between types of certainty made its first appearance in Western thought with Aristotle's *Nichomachean Ethics*. He says that for different fields of knowledge, we should expect different types of certainty: "In the same spirit, therefore, should each type of statement be received; for it is the mark of an educated man to look for precision in each class of things just so far as the nature of the subject admits; it is evidently equally foolish to accept probable reasoning from a mathematician and to demand from a rhetorician scientific proofs."[1] It would make no sense to require mathematical certainty from something other than math, and it would be unreasonable to accept from a mathematician anything but mathematical certainty.

St. Thomas Aquinas further develops the concept of certainty by applying it to faith. In the *Summa Theologiae*, he poses the question: "Whether faith is more certain than knowledge and the other intellectual virtues?" He says that the content of faith in one sense is more certain because it is revealed by God, and God is the source of all truth.

In the subjective sense, St. Thomas states that faith is less certain, as it is beyond our understanding and our full grasp. To illustrate his point, he uses the image of someone with little knowledge trusting the words of an expert. Although the eyes of the person with little knowledge may not be able to fully grasp what is happening, the person trusts the words of the expert who explains the phenomenon to him.[2] For the person with little knowledge, the information is reasonably certain only if he is certain that the person speaking is an expert and that he properly understood the expert. For Catholics, we have the undoubtable certainty of faith whenever the Church pronounces a certain dogma

1   Aristotle, *Nicomachean Ethics I, 3,* trans. W. D. Ross, accessed December 31, 2020, http://classics.mit.edu/Aristotle/nicomachaen .html.

2   Thomas Aquinas, *Summa Theologiae II-II, a. 4, q. 8.*

or doctrine. We are certain that God speaks through the Church, so we have the highest level of certainty regarding our faith.

In the first section of this work, we assume that the reader has accepted the Bible as divinely revealed. This section uses the historical and literary evidence found within the Bible to clarify what God meant by the inspired Word. The second section continues the argument of the first section but adds the evidence provided by the Fathers of the Church. It uses the same tools of historical and literary analysis to examine the Fathers' writings. The purpose of the first two sections is to present enough historical and literary evidence to convince someone beyond a reasonable doubt that God has revealed the doctrine of the Real Presence as understood by the Catholic Church. The third section of the book takes a different approach; it examines purported Eucharistic miracles through the eyes of science, requiring unique evidence and a distinct method separate from the first two sections in an attempt to arrive at scientific certainty.

On Structure

We divided the book into three sections according to the evidence that we use to argue for the Real Presence of Christ in the Eucharist. The first section uses Scripture to argue for a holistic and contextual reading of the Bible that points to Jesus meaning what He said at the Last Supper: "This is my body" and "This is . . . my blood." However, the biblical section's weakness is twofold: first, to believe arguments from the Bible, one has to believe the Bible. For non-Christians, this section will not be convincing. Also, as anyone who has done some apologetic work knows, the unsystematic nature of the Bible allows for different interpretations of the same passage depending on the hermeneutic or presuppositions with which one approaches the Scriptures. For someone who doesn't think that the Scriptures should be read as a united whole, such that each passage should be read contextually, the arguments in the first section of this book will not be convincing.

For that reason, we added the second section on the early Fathers of the Church. The Fathers of the Church are the early Christian saints and theologians. The earliest Fathers of the Church learned directly from the apostles themselves, or from their disciples. Therefore, the earliest Fathers proximity to our Lord makes their witness all the more compelling. Within one generation, a person's teachings can only mutate so much. The discipleship system at the time of Christ makes the Church Father's teachings even more convincing. The disciple's role was to memorize, internalize, and live the teaching of the master so that the teachings of a master could be preserved for many generations. And so, what the first several centuries of Christians believed is what Jesus taught. For us as Catholics, the Fathers of the Church are even more convincing because we believe that Jesus Christ sent His Holy Spirit to guide the Church to all truth, just as the Fathers of the Church were also guided and aided by the Holy Spirit. These two sections should be sufficient to convince someone with faith that Jesus Christ is really and truly present in the Eucharist.

The third section of this book examines three of the most well-known reports of alleged Eucharistic miracles:

Bolsena in 1263, Buenos Aires in the 1990s, and Lanciano in the 700s, including a review of the famous Linoli Report. The historical accounts and scientific findings of these miracles as they were presented to the local episcopacy have been reviewed critically. In these events, the bread was claimed to have turned into heart tissue and the wine into blood. Since today these approved investigations are offered as evidence for the Real Presence of Christ in the Eucharist, we judge that a careful appraisal both for and against the scientific claims is necessary. More than ever, this is a time to assert that the claims of scientific findings are rarely absolute. Belief in science can never be as certain as faith in Christ. The data from these reports, which for various reasons is inconclusive, begs the ultimate question of the certainty of faith. Is it more reasonable to place faith in the experiments and analytical methods of man or the words of Christ? The reader may be joyfully surprised at where the journey of this book will lead.

PART I

WHAT DOES THE BIBLE SAY?

1

THE WHOLE STORY:
THE OLD TESTAMENT PASSAGES

Introduction

WHEN speaking to non-Catholic Christians about the Eucharist, Catholics often cite John chapter 6 and the institution narratives as definitive proofs that the Eucharist is truly Jesus's flesh and blood. While those are the most powerful biblical passages supporting the Real Presence, we need to point out the Old Testament foundation first. To the average Protestant, there is no way that Jesus meant something as bold as the Catholic claim concerning the Eucharist when, according to their understanding, John 6 and the Last Supper are the only passages that even hint at the Eucharist throughout the Scriptures.

Their point of view is understandable. Why would something of such monumental importance appear in such an isolated way? Why would God not prepare His people for such a gift through prefigurements and images throughout the Old Testament? Why do we not see this as a central part of the early Church's life? In the Old Testament, we can see preparations for the other great gifts of God in Jesus Christ, and the New Testament frequently talks about these great gifts too. Why not this one?

The truth is that the Old Testament texts do prefigure the Eucharist several times, and the New Testament records the early Christians celebrating the Eucharist. In this chapter, we'll look at those prefigurements and references to the Eucharist in the Old Testament.

Types and Prefigurements

Before we dive into the biblical types or prefigurements of the Eucharist, it would be good to define what we mean by those words. The word "type" comes from the Greek word τύπος (*typos*), which had an original meaning of "stamp" or "imprint," such as the imprint used to mark coins with the image of the emperor. The word also developed to mean a foreshadowing or preparation for a similar but different thing to come. The term "prefigurement" draws its root from *figura,* which is the Latin translation of the Greek word τύπος (*typos*). For our purposes, the words "type" and "prefigurement" will be completely interchangeable.

The *Catholic Encyclopedia* defines a type as "a person, a thing, or an action, having its own independent and absolute existence, but at the same time intended by God to prefigure a future person, thing, or action."[1] So, when we speak of Old Testament types, we are indicating persons, things, or actions that truly existed or happened in the Old Testament which God, in His wisdom and providence, ordained to exist at that time to prepare His people for the fulfillment to be revealed in Jesus Christ. In simpler terms, biblical types are like road signs or movie trailers that point us to, or give us a taste of, what is to come.

---

1   *The Catholic Encyclopedia, Volume XV,* s.v., "type."

The use of prefigurements to understand the Bible is not a recent invention of the Church. From the very beginning, God intended the use of types and prefigurements to understand the Old Testament. They were used by the authors of the New Testament and by the early Christians. For example, in Romans 5:14, St. Paul refers to Adam as "a type of the one who was to come," Christ being the one who was to come. In 1 Peter 3:21, the flood in the time of Noah is referred to as a prefigurement (ἀντίτυπον, *antitypon*) of Baptism. The author of the Letter to the Hebrews laced the text with typological interpretations of the Old Testament priesthood, temple, and sacrifices pointing to Christ's eternal priesthood and sacrifice.[2] In St. Ignatius of Antioch's letters (ca. AD 100), traces of types are used, and St. Justin Martyr's *Dialogue with Trypho* (written ca. AD 150) deals mostly with how the Old Testament prefigures and prophesies Jesus Christ, the New Covenant, and the Church. Other early Christian writers, such as Origen (c. 184–254), St. Hilary of Poitiers (300–368), St. Ambrose (340–397), and St. Augustine (345–430), explicitly and widely use typology to interpret the Scriptures. Also, the earliest Christians used types and prefigurements to interpret the Scriptures; therefore, it's reasonable for us to interpret the New Testament in light of Old Testament prefigurements. In this chapter, we'll look at the tree of life, the sacrifice of Melchizedek, the Passover, the manna, and the bread of Presence and how each foreshadowed the Eucharist.

---

2   Cf. Heb 4:14–5:10; 7:11–10:18.

The Tree of Life

Genesis chapter 2 introduces the tree of life: "And out of
the ground the LORD God made to grow every tree that is
pleasant to the sight and good for food, the tree of life also
in the midst of the garden, and the tree of the knowledge
of good and evil" (Gn 2:9). Genesis 3:22 provides more
details regarding the tree: "Behold, the man has become
like one of us, knowing good and evil; and now, lest he put
forth his hand and take also of the tree of life, and eat, and
live for ever." So, the tree of life was a particular tree in the
Garden of Eden (note: it's a different tree than the tree of
the knowledge of good and evil!), Adam and Eve were permitted to eat of the fruit of the tree of life (see Gn 2:16–17)
when they were in the right relationship with God (see Gn
3:24), and the effect of eating the fruit of the tree was living
forever. All three of those points foreshadow the Eucharist:

1. The Eucharist is not ordinary bread but a particular kind of food (cf. 1 Cor 11:29).
2. Those who are in a right relationship with God
   by being in the state of grace and fully members
   of the Universal Church are permitted to eat the
   Eucharist (cf. 1 Cor 11:27).
3. As St. Ignatius of Antioch wrote in his letters to
   the Ephesians, the Eucharist is the "medicine of
   immortality, the antidote we take in order not to
   die but to live forever in Jesus Christ"[3] (cf. Jn
   6:58).

---

3   Ignatius, *Letter to the Ephesians*, 20.

The Eucharist is the food of eternal life, only received by those in a right relationship with God, and results in a share in everlasting life, much like the tree of life in the Garden of Eden.

The Sacrifice of Melchizedek

Melchizedek only appears a few times in the Old Testament, but the author of the Letter to the Hebrews understands him as one of the principal prefigurements of Jesus Christ the High Priest (see Heb 7). To comprehend how his sacrifice foreshadows the Eucharist, we'll start by reviewing what we know about Melchizedek from the Old Testament.

Genesis 14:17–20 says, "After [Abraham's] return from the defeat of Ched-or-lao'mer and the kings who were with him, the king of Sodom went out to meet him at the Valley of Sha'veh (that is, the King's Valley). And Melchiz'edek king of Salem brought out bread and wine; he was priest of God Most High. And he blessed him and said, 'Blessed be Abram by God Most High, / maker of heaven and earth; / and blessed be God Most High, / who has delivered your enemies into your hand!' And Abram gave him a tenth of everything."

Melchizedek appears again in Psalm 110:4: "The LORD has sworn / and will not change his mind, / 'You are a priest for ever / according to the order of Melchiz'edek.'"

From these two passages, we can extract four points about Melchizedek:

1. He offered bread and wine.
2. He blessed Abraham.
3. Abraham tithed to Melchizedek.
4. Melchizedek's priesthood was a priesthood that would last forever.

Hebrews chapter 7 connects the priesthood of Melchizedek to the priesthood of Jesus through points two through four. It says that Jesus's priesthood is a higher priesthood than the Levitical priesthood, similar to how Melchizedek's priesthood is higher than the Levitical priesthood. Why was Melchizedek's priesthood higher than the Levitical priesthood? Because of points two and three. The higher priest blesses the lower, and the lower tithes to the higher. So, if Abraham had a lower priesthood than Melchizedek, and the Levites came from Abraham, then Melchizedek had a higher priesthood than the Levitical priesthood. Point four connects Melchizedek's unending priesthood with Jesus Christ, the High Priest who lives forever.

The key to interpreting the sacrifice of Melchizedek as a type of the Eucharist is understanding that the *priesthood* of Melchizedek specifically prefigures the *priesthood* of Jesus. What do priests do? They offer sacrifice. If one priesthood prefigures another priesthood, then one sacrifice prefigures the other sacrifice. Therefore, the sacrifice of the bread and wine offered by Melchizedek prefigures the sacrifice of Jesus Christ offered at the Last Supper.

Passover

"Behold the Lamb of God, who takes away the sin of the world!" (Jn 1:29). These words shouted by John the Baptist at the beginning of Jesus's public ministry would have seemed a bit out of place. The crowds at the Jordan River were there to receive a baptism of repentance,[4] but when

---

4   John's baptism was essentially being washed by water as an outward
sign of one's commitment to change one's life and be cleansed of past
sins.

Jesus appears, John starts talking about a sacrificial lamb. He even does this a second time the next day when Jesus calls his disciples (see Jn 1:36). Here's the problem: there was nothing resembling a sacrifice happening at the Jordan River. Sacrifices happened far away in the Jerusalem Temple. Why would John call Jesus a lamb at that time, the very first moment of His public ministry? The only reasonable answer is because the Lamb of God prefigured Jesus in a meaningful way, which was essential for the disciples' knowledge of Jesus's ministry from the very beginning.

To understand what it means that Jesus is the new Lamb of God, we have to understand the old lamb of God: the Passover lamb. The Passover was the sacrifice that God commanded the Israelites to offer before He would lead them out of Egypt. God had sent nine plagues upon Egypt. The Israelites had to suffer the nine plagues with the Egyptians, but the tenth and last plague was too awful for God to allow the Israelites to suffer: the death of the firstborn. After being slaughtered, the blood of the Passover lamb was sprinkled on the house doorsteps and later consumed. This was the outward sign that prevented the firstborn from losing his life. Here is the passage from Exodus that describes the Passover lamb's sacrifice and meal:

> The LORD said to Moses and Aaron in the land of Egypt, "This month shall be for you the beginning of months; it shall be the first month of the year for you. . . . Your lamb shall be without blemish, a male a year old; you shall take it from the sheep or from the goats; and you shall keep it until the fourteenth day of this month, when the whole assembly of the congregation of Israel shall kill their lambs in the evening. Then they shall take some of the blood, and put it on the two doorposts and the lintel of the houses in which they eat them. They shall eat the flesh that night, roasted. . . . This day shall be for you a

memorial day, and you shall keep it as a feast to the LORD;
throughout your generations you shall observe it as an
ordinance for ever. (Ex 12:1–2, 5–8, 14)

From this passage, we can draw out three points that are
important for our study:

1. The Passover lamb was to be unblemished.
2. The Passover lamb was killed and eaten on the
   same day.
3. The Passover was to be a memorial day every
   year and was to be a sacrifice offered forever.

Since the Passover lamb was a liturgical celebration offered
every year, the rite slowly developed over time to explain
and expand what the nucleus text in Exodus commanded. A
few of those changes are worth noting for the sake of understanding how the Passover lamb prefigures the Eucharist.
The book of Deuteronomy records the first development:
"You may not offer the Passover sacrifice within any of your
towns which the LORD your God gives you; but at the place
which the LORD your God will choose, to make his name
dwell in it, there you shall offer the Passover sacrifice, in the
evening at the going down of the sun, at the time you came
out of Egypt. And you shall boil it and eat it at the place
which the LORD your God will choose; and in the morning
you shall turn and go to your tents" (Dt 16:5–7).

The Israelites celebrated the first Passover in the houses
of each of the families, but when the people of Israel
entered the promised land, they were to offer the Passover
"at the place which the Lord your God will choose, to make

his name dwell in it," meaning the tent of meeting (cf. Ex 40:34) and then the Jerusalem Temple (cf. 2 Chr 5:14). Also, this passage refers to the Passover as a sacrifice, making it clear that the Passover is primarily a sacrifice and then a meal.

The second difference is quite fascinating. Before the lamb was roasted as sacrifice, vertical and horizontal skewers were run through the lamb's flesh, forming the shape of a cross.[5] St. Justin Martyr, a second-century Christian martyr, refers to this in his work *Dialogue with Trypho the Jew* when he says about the Passover lamb, "For the lamb, which is roasted, is roasted and dressed up in the form of the cross."[6]

Therefore, we can add to the above list two additional points that are important for our study:

1. The Passover was celebrated in Jerusalem.
2. The Passover lambs were sacrificed using a wooden instrument in the form of a cross.

With these points, we can now look at Jesus Christ and examine how He is the new Lamb of God. Here is an outline of the prefigurement:

---

5   (see Pesachim 5, 9; 7, 1)
6   Justin Martyr, *Dialogue with Trypho,* Ch. 40.

Passover Lamb	Jesus
1. Unblemished lamb	No sin or broken bones
2. Killed and eaten on the same day	Last Supper and Crucifixion on the same day (in the Jewish calendar)
3. Commanded to be a memorial	Commanded to "Do this in memory"
4. In Jerusalem	In Jerusalem
5. Immolated on a wooden cross	Killed on a wooden cross

The Passover's regulation that the lamb be unblemished meant essentially that the lamb could not have any birth defects or damage done to it after birth (such as broken bones). Jesus Christ was the unblemished lamb, both morally and bodily. Jesus committed no sin, and therefore was morally unblemished: "He committed no sin, and no guile was found on his lips" (1 Pt 2:22; cf. Is 53:9). Also, the New Testament repeatedly emphasizes Jesus's purity (see 1 Cor 5:21; Heb 4:15; 1 Jn 3:5). The Roman soldiers chose not to break His legs like those of the other two they crucified with Him (see Jn 19:32), keeping Him unblemished even in His body. For this reason, 1 Peter 1:18–19 says, "You know that you were ransomed from the futile ways inherited from your fathers, not with perishable things such as silver or gold, but with the precious blood of Christ, like that of a lamb without blemish or spot."

The second point is difficult to understand for the modern reader due to the difference in the Jewish calendar's and the current Gregorian calendar's ways of measuring days. Unlike our calendar, the Jewish calendar's day started at sundown and ended at the following sundown. So, for example, a single Jewish day would start on the Gregorian calendar's Thursday evening and then end on the Gregorian calendar's Friday evening. This was the case with Jesus's last supper and crucifixion. The Last Supper happened in the evening on Thursday, and then Jesus was crucified in the mid-afternoon on the same Jewish day (the Gregorian calendar's Friday). Therefore, the Last Supper and the Crucifixion happened on the same day, just as the sacrifice of the lamb and the Passover meal were on the same day.

The last three points are straightforward. Exodus 12:14 says that the Passover shall be a remembrance, and at the Last Supper, Jesus commanded the apostles to "do this in remembrance of me" (Lk 22:19; 1 Cor 11:24). The Passover was celebrated in Jerusalem, where the Last Supper occurred, and the Crucifixion happened right outside the walls of Jerusalem (because Roman executions at that time were not permitted inside the city's walls). The Passover lambs were killed and immolated on a wooden cross. Jesus was crucified on a wooden cross.

The linchpin to the Passover being a type of the Eucharist is highlighting the necessity of *eating the Passover lamb*. Many non-Catholics will concede that the Passover foreshadows the Crucifixion, but they do not acknowledge that the Eucharist is how we eat the new Lamb of God. As we saw above, the Passover was a two-part ritual: the slaughtering of the lambs and the Passover meal. The Scriptures are clear: the eating of the Passover lamb is essential. Paul references the important connection between eating the sacrifice and the fruits of the sacrifice in 1 Corinthians

10:18, "Consider the people of Israel; are not those who eat the sacrifices partners in the altar?" To make the point more clearly, in Exodus 12:1–28, the passage in which God explains to the Israelites how to celebrate the Passover, God refers to slaughtering the lamb only two times, while He mentions eating the lamb seven times. The directions for how to, when to, and who can eat the lamb are far more extensive than how to slaughter the lamb. And lastly, in Exodus, God commands the Israelites two times to kill the lamb, but He commands them to eat it four times. From a scriptural point of view, the slaughtering of the lamb is arguably a necessity only to get to the more important Passover meal.

For the salvation wrought by Jesus, He used a two-part ritual as well: the Last Supper in which the apostles ate the body of the new Lamb of God and the slaughtering of the new Lamb on a cross. There is a clear parallel between the slaughtering of the Passover lamb and Christ's crucifixion. Likewise, there is a clear parallel between the Passover meal and the Eucharist. If eating the flesh of the lamb was essential to the sacrifice of Passover, then eating the flesh of the new Lamb of God in the Eucharist is essential to the sacrifice of Jesus Christ. Therefore, the Passover lamb foreshadows Jesus in the Eucharist.

The Manna

After the Jews celebrated the Passover and escaped into the desert, God gave us another prefigurement of the Eucharist: the manna in the wilderness. Exodus 16:13–15 describes the manna for the first time: "In the morning dew lay round about the camp. And when the dew had gone up, there was on the face of the wilderness a fine, flake-like thing, fine as hoarfrost on the ground. When the sons of Israel saw it, they said to one another, 'What is it?' For they did not know what it was. And Moses said to them, 'It is the bread that the LORD has given you to eat.'"

The manna in the desert prefigures the Eucharist in three ways: Firstly, because it is the bread come down from heaven (see Ps 78:24). Jesus makes this parallel clear in John 6:48–51 when He says, "I am the bread of life. Your fathers ate the manna in the wilderness, and they died. This is the bread which comes down from heaven, that a man may eat of it and not die. I am the living bread which came down from heaven."

Secondly, the manna was not a fruit of the labor of humanity. It was a gift from God. Likewise, God's gift of Himself to us in the Eucharist is totally gratuitous.

Thirdly, God gave the Israelites the gift of manna every morning to sustain them as they wandered in the desert. When they reached the Promised Land, the gift of manna stopped. So also, the Eucharist is given to us while we are wayfarers in this life. When we reach God willingly, we will no longer receive the Eucharist because we will have entered into our promised heavenly homeland, and we will be united to Christ eternally.

The Bread of Presence

The bread of Presence is best known from the Old Testament scene when David and his companions are fleeing Saul and they are permitted to eat the bread in the temple:

24 BEHOLD, IT IS I

The priest answered David, "I have no common bread at hand, but there is holy bread; if only the young men have kept themselves from women." And David answered the priest, "Of a truth women have been kept from us as always when I go on an expedition; the vessels of the young men are holy, even when it is a common journey; how much more today will their vessels be holy?" So the priest gave him the holy bread; for there was no bread there except the bread of the Presence, which is removed from before the LORD, to be replaced by hot bread on the day it is taken away. (1 Sm 21:4–6)

Citing the above scene to the Pharisees, Jesus explains why it is acceptable for His disciples to pluck the heads of grain from the field as they pass through on the sabbath: "He said to them, 'Have you not read what David did when he was hungry, and those who were with him: how he entered the house of God and ate the showbread, which it was not lawful for him to eat nor for those who were with him, but only for the priests? Or have you not read in the law how on the sabbath the priests in the temple profane the sabbath, and are guiltless? I tell you, something greater than the temple is here'" (Mt 12:3–6).

The statement "I tell you, something greater than the temple is here" is significant. When Jesus makes the parallel between Himself and the temple and goes on to state that He is greater than the temple, Jesus is saying that He is the perfection, or completion, of the temple and all of its sacrifices. We have already spoken about how the sacrifice of the Passover lamb prefigures Jesus. The bread of Presence is also a prefigurement of the Eucharistic sacrifice.

Exodus 25:30 first mentions the bread of Presence, "And you shall set the bread of the Presence on the table before me always." But the details are fleshed out in Leviticus 24:5–9:

You shall take fine flour, and bake twelve cakes of it; two-tenths of an ephah shall be in each cake. And you shall set them in two rows, six in a row, upon the table of pure gold. And you shall put pure frankincense with each row, that it may go with the bread as a memorial portion to be offered by fire to the Lord. Every sabbath day Aaron shall set it in order before the Lord continually on behalf of the sons of Israel as a covenant for ever. And it shall be for Aaron and his sons, and they shall eat it in a holy place, since it is for him a most holy portion out of the offerings by fire to the Lord, a perpetual debt.

The details to draw out of this passage are that this bread is set out "as a covenant for ever," it is a "memorial portion," and the loaves of bread were reserved for the priests because "it is for him a most holy portion." The Eucharist parallels the bread of the presence on all three points: Firstly, at the Last Supper, Jesus calls the Eucharist the "the new covenant" (Lk 22:20; 1 Cor 11:25). Secondly, the apostles are commanded to "do this in remembrance of me" (Lk 22:19). Thirdly, only those who have been baptized into Christ's priesthood can receive the Eucharist, just as only the priests were permitted to eat the bread of Presence.

Review/Summary

Key Ideas

- The Old Testament contains many prefigurements of the Eucharist stretching from Genesis up to the time of Christ.
- The fruit of the tree of life, the sacrifice of Melchizedek, the Passover, the manna in the wilderness, and the bread of Presence are all prefigurements of the Eucharist.

Good Facts to Memorize

- Genesis 2:9 and 3:22 contain the passages on the tree of life.
- Genesis 14:17–20 describes Melchizedek, and Hebrews 7 connects Melchizedek to Jesus.
- The Passover lamb *had to be eaten*. Go to Exodus 12:1–28 for the proof text.
- Exodus 16:14–15 is the first appearance of the manna in the desert. John 6 connects the manna to the Eucharist.

Effective Questions to Ask When Discussing the Real Presence

- It was necessary to eat the fruit of the tree of life, the Passover lamb, and the manna to be saved. If we do not eat Jesus, who is the new tree of life, the new Lamb of God, and the new bread from heaven in the Eucharist, then how does He save us?
- Why was eating of the fruit, the Passover lamb, and the manna so important in the Old Testament? Why do some claim that it is not necessary anymore?

2

THE INSTITUTION NARRATIVES

Introduction

"ON the day before he was to suffer, he took bread in his holy and venerable hands, and with eyes raised to heaven to you, O God, his almighty Father, giving you thanks, he said the blessing, broke the bread and gave it to his disciples, saying: Take this, all of you, and eat of it, for this is my Body."[1] With these words, the Catholic Church memorializes, offers, celebrates, and makes present Jesus Christ in the Eucharist. The group of biblical texts called the institution narratives are the texts that recount the words of Jesus when He instituted the Eucharist on the night of the Last Supper. Three of them are in the Gospels of Matthew, Mark, and Luke, and one is in Paul's First Letter to the Corinthians. These are essential texts in the apologist's toolbox to defend the Catholic Church's teaching on the Real Presence of Christ in the Eucharist. They have some minor variations, and each line is rich with meaning, so it is worth it to look at all four texts in detail.

---

1   Roman Missal, Eucharistic Prayer I, n. 89.

The Texts

Matthew 26:26–29: "As they were eating, Jesus took bread, and blessed, and broke it, and gave it to the disciples, and said, 'Take, eat; this is my body.' And he took a chalice, and after giving thanks he gave it to them, saying, 'Drink of it, all of you; for this is my blood of the covenant, which is poured out for many for the forgiveness of sins. I tell you I shall not drink again of this fruit of the vine until that day when I drink it new with you in my Father's kingdom.'"

Mark 14:22–25: "As they were eating, he took bread, and blessed, and broke it, gave it to them, and said, 'Take; this is my body.' And he took a chalice, and when he had given thanks he gave it to them, and they all drank of it. He said to them, 'This is my blood of the covenant, which is poured out for many. Truly I say to you, I shall not again drink of the fruit of the vine until that day when I drink it new in the kingdom of God.'"

Luke 22:14–20: "When the hour came, he sat at table, and the apostles with him. And he said to them, 'I have earnestly desired to eat this Passover with you before I suffer; for I tell you, I shall not eat it until it is fulfilled in the kingdom of God.' Then he took a chalice, and when he had given thanks he said, 'Take this, and divide it among yourselves; for I tell you that from now on I will not drink of the fruit of the vine until the kingdom of God comes.' Then he took bread, and when he had given thanks he broke it and gave it to them, saying, 'This is my body, which is given for you. Do this in remembrance of me.' And likewise the chalice after supper, saying, 'This chalice that is poured out for you is the new covenant in my blood.'"

1 Corinthians 11:23–26: "For I received from the Lord what I also delivered to you, that the Lord Jesus on the night when he was betrayed took bread, and when he had given thanks, he broke it, and said, 'This is my body which is for you. Do this in remembrance of me.' In the same way also the chalice, after supper, saying, 'This chalice is the new covenant in my blood. Do this, as often as you drink it, in remembrance of me.' For as often as you eat this bread and drink the chalice, you proclaim the Lord's death until he comes."

At First Glance

Several features stand out from the institution narratives. First, they all have substantially the same content: on the night before He died, Jesus took bread and said, "this is my body," then He took the wine and said, "this is my blood." It's clear that all four passages are recounting the same moment in Jesus's life and that they all record the same words of Jesus. In the Scriptures, that is rare. We have very few moments in Christ's life that are recorded four times in the New Testament. Think about it: His birth appears only twice in the Scriptures, His first miracle at the wedding at Cana only once, the Sermon on the Mount only once, and the raising of Lazarus only once. Even the most significant scenes of Jesus's life don't often have the same words recounted. Think of the Crucifixion, the Resurrection, and the Ascension. The authors of the Scriptures record them multiple times, but they choose different sayings of Jesus to pass down through their writings. But that is not the case with the Last Supper. We have four accounts of the same scene and essentially the same words in all four. Therefore, this scene and these words were understood by the early Church to be extremely important.

Despite the wording being substantially identical, the differences merit some attention. Matthew and Mark record the scene with almost the same vocabulary, with Matthew adding the lines "for the forgiveness of sins" and the explanatory "eat" and "with you" and then using "my Father" instead of Mark's "God" at the end of the cited passage.

Underlined Text Is Variant Words of Christ in Matthew and Mark	
Matthew	**Mark**
"As they were eating, Jesus took bread, and blessed, and broke it, and gave it to the disciples, and said, '**Take, <u>eat</u>; this is my body.**' And he took a chalice, and after giving thanks he gave it to them, saying, '**<u>Drink of it, all of you; for</u> this is my blood of the covenant, which is poured out for many <u>for the forgiveness of sins</u>. I tell you I shall not drink again of this fruit of the vine until that day when I drink it new <u>with you</u> in <u>my Father's</u> kingdom.**'"	"As they were eating, he took bread, and blessed, and broke it, gave it to them, and said, '**Take; this is my body.**' And he took a chalice, and when he had given thanks he gave it to them, and they all drank of it. He said to them, '**This is my blood of the covenant, which is poured out for many. <u>Truly</u> I say to you, I shall not again drink of the fruit of the vine until that day when I drink it new in the kingdom <u>of God</u>.**'"

As seen above, the vast majority of the text aligns perfectly with only a few variable sections.

The Gospel of Luke and Paul's First Letter to the Corinthians similarly use almost the same wording for Jesus's statements.

Underlined Text Is Variant Words of Christ in Luke and Paul	
Luke	**Paul**
"Then [Jesus] took bread, and when he had given thanks he broke it and gave it to them, saying, **'This is my body, which is <u>given</u> for you. Do this in remembrance of me.'** And likewise the chalice after supper, saying, **'This chalice <u>that is poured out for you</u> is the new covenant in my blood.'"**	"For I received from the Lord what I also delivered to you, that the Lord Jesus on the night when he was betrayed took bread, and when he had given thanks, he broke it, and said, **'This is my body which is for you. Do this in remembrance of me.'** In the same way also the chalice, after supper, saying, **'This chalice is the new covenant in my blood. <u>Do this, as often as you drink it, in remembrance of me.'"</u>**

Luke simply clarifies that the body is "given" and that the chalice "is poured out for you," and Paul adds the command to "do this" after the consecration of the chalice.

Many scholars conclude that there were at least two prevalent traditions that preserved the words of Jesus on that night. One tradition was the Matthew-Mark tradition, which handed on the phrasing "take . . . this is my body" and "this is my blood of the covenant which is poured out."

The other tradition was the Luke-Paul tradition, which was "this is my body . . . for you" and "this chalice . . . is the new covenant in my blood."

Variant Words of Christ in Matthew-Mark and Luke-Paul Traditions *Using the longer variant from each tradition*	
Matthew-Mark	**Luke-Paul**
"Take, eat; this is my body."	"This is my body, which is given for you. Do this in remembrance of me."
"Drink of it, all of you; for this is my blood of the covenant, which is poured out for many for the forgiveness of sins. I tell you I shall not drink again of this fruit of the vine until that day when I drink it new with you in my Father's kingdom."	"This chalice is the new covenant in my blood. Do this, as often as you drink it, in remembrance of me."

The differences in wording are easily reconcilable. The words of Jesus are recorded in a different order, there are some omissions, and there are some summaries of longer phrases. In the consecration of the bread, the Matthew-Mark tradition adds "take, eat" at the beginning, and the Luke-Paul tradition adds "which is given for you. Do this in remembrance of me" at the end. In the consecration of the chalice, once again the Matthew-Mark tradition adds the command beforehand, "Drink from it, all of you," and the lines about forgiveness of sins and not drinking the fruit of the vine again at the end. The Luke-Paul tradition adds "do this, as often as you drink it, in remembrance of me" to the end. The words of consecration for the blood themselves are harder to reconcile. In Matthew and Mark, Jesus says, "This is my blood of the covenant," and in Luke and Paul, our Lord says, "This chalice is the new covenant in my blood." The exact wording is difficult to pin down, but both traditions preserve the core concepts "this is my blood" and "this is the blood of the covenant."

"Prepare the Passover"

Before each of the Last Supper accounts in the Synoptic Gospels (Matthew, Mark, and Luke), Jesus commands His disciples to prepare for Him and His disciples to eat the Passover (see Mt 26:17–19; Mk 14:12–16; Lk 22:7–13). That evening, they eat the Passover. However, this Passover is somewhat different: Jesus seems to follow the ritual of the Passover left to us by the rabbis of Jesus's time up through the second cup. For a better understanding of this section, review the portion of the previous chapter called "Passover."

In the Passover meal at Jesus's time, there were four cups. The first cup was called the cup of sanctification, over which the head of the household would say a formal blessing. The Jews called the second cup the cup of proclamation, because, after the mixing of the second cup, the father would proclaim what God had done and would explain the meaning of the night and the different parts of the meal.

At the third cup, the Last Supper seems to take a path of
its own. Dr. Brant Pitre summarizes well the steps of the
third cup according to Jewish tradition:

> It probably consisted of at least three basic steps. First, a
> blessing would have been said over the unleavened bread,
> before beginning the meal. The standard Jewish blessing went
> something like this: "Blessed are you, Lord God, who brings
> forth bread from the earth" (see Mishnah, Berakoth 6:1).
> Second, the meal probably began with the serving of an hors
> d'oeuvre, consisting of a small morsel of bread dipped in the
> bowl of sauce. This morsel is referred to in the Mishnah as
> a kind of appetizer. It may also have been the "morsel" that
> Judas dipped in the "dish" before leaving the Last Supper to
> betray Jesus (John 13:26–27). Third, after the appetizer, the
> main meal would have been eaten, consisting primarily of
> unleavened bread and the flesh of the Passover lamb. Once the
> meal itself was finished, the father would say another blessing
> over the third cup of wine. The third cup was known as the cup
> of blessing – in Hebrew, the barakah cup. When this cup was
> drunk, the third stage of the Passover supper was complete.[2]

As far as we can tell, Jesus followed the ritual of the Passover through the dipping of the morsel, but when the main
course came along, He deviated from the custom. At the
eating of the unleavened bread, Jesus does something new,
unexpected, and unprecedented. For when Jesus speaks,
His words become reality: "This is my body." Interestingly,
the flesh of the Passover lamb is ordinarily eaten at this
time as well, but no mention is made of the lamb. While it
may have simply been omitted because it was not essential
to the recounting of the Last Supper, it is fitting that the
old lamb of God would not be eaten because the flesh of

---

2   Brant Pitre, *Jesus and the Jewish Roots of the Eucharist: Unlocking
     the Secrets of the Last Supper* (New York: Image, 2016), p. 155.

Jesus, the new Lamb of God, had fulfilled and replaced it. Regardless of whether Jesus and the apostles ate the flesh of the Passover lamb, the Gospel writers considered the words and actions of Jesus concerning the unleavened bread and wine to dwarf the eating of the flesh of the Passover lamb.

The fourth cup was called the cup of praise (heb. *hallel*). The ritual for the fourth cup started after dinner was completed and the third cup had been received. They would sing Psalms 115 to 118, which, when sung together, were known as the Great Hallel. Then they would drink the fourth cup, signifying the end of the Passover meal. At this fourth cup, Jesus seriously deviates from the ordinary Passover ritual. Sacred Scripture says the following:

> And likewise the chalice after supper, saying, "This chalice that is poured out for you is the new covenant in my blood." (Lk 22:20)

> And he took a chalice, and after giving thanks he gave it to them, saying, "Drink of it, all of you; for this is my blood of the covenant, which is poured out for many for the forgiveness of sins. I tell you I shall not drink again of this fruit of the vine until that day when I drink it new with you in my Father's kingdom." And when they had sung a hymn, they went out to the Mount of Olives. (Mt 26:27–30)

> And he took a chalice, and when he had given thanks he gave it to them, and they all drank of it. He said to them, "This is my blood of the covenant, which is poured out for many. Truly I say to you, I shall not again drink of the fruit of the vine until that day when I drink it new in the kingdom of God." And when they had sung a hymn, they went out to the Mount of Olives. (Mk 14:23–26)

Luke mentions that the chalice over which Jesus pronounces the words of consecration is the cup "after supper," also known as the third cup. Matthew and Mark say that after the third cup, Jesus and His disciples sang a hymn, which is agreed by most scholars to be the Great Hallel (Ps 115–118).

But Jesus seems to have forgotten something: there is no mention of drinking the fourth cup. "And when they had sung a hymn, they went out to the Mount of Olives" (Mt 26:30; Mk 14:26). Forgetting the fourth cup would be baffling to a Jew at the time of Jesus. How could Jesus, a thirty-three-year-old devout Jew, forget the fourth cup? His words after the consecration of the third cup explain that it was no mistake: "Truly I say to you, I shall not again drink of the fruit of the vine until that day when I drink it new in the kingdom of God." Jesus intentionally extended His new Passover meal through His passion and death all the way to the heavenly kingdom of God. This point is crucial because it means that for Jesus, the cross and Last Supper are one sacrifice. At the cross, the new Lamb of God was slaughtered, and at the Last Supper, the new Lamb of God was ritually offered and eaten. If this essential truth is understood and believed, then the Old Testament prefigurements, John's bread of life discourse, Paul's passages on the Lord's Supper in First Corinthians, and the Letter to the Hebrews can be accurately understood and interpreted regarding the Eucharist.

In summary, there are three main points to keep in mind in this section: Firstly, the Passover meal that Jesus offered with His disciples was different from the customary Passover meal because Jesus intended to establish a new Passover. Secondly, Jesus makes the meal different by introducing Himself into the meal as our food. The lamb of the old Passover rite cedes its place to Jesus, the Lamb of

God. Thirdly, Jesus intentionally extends the Passover meal through His passion and death and into heaven because He wants us to understand it all as one unified mystery.

What Does "Is" Mean?

Due to a lack of faith, and partly due to the complicated nature of language, many people doubt that Jesus meant what He said in regards to the Eucharist. A thorough apologetic presentation merits a clarification on the meaning of "is" in the words of Jesus: "This is my body" and "This is the chalice of my blood."

Thankfully, biblical scholars have thoroughly researched not only the roots of the Greek words but even the likely Aramaic words that Jesus would have used at the Last Supper. The English translations that we have are faithful translations of the New Testament Greek text. The Greek τοῦτό ἐστιν τὸ σῶμά μου (Koine: *touto estin to soma mou*) translates literally to "this is my body," and the Greek τοῦτο γάρ ἐστιν τὸ αἷμά μου (Koine: *touto gar estin to haima mou*) translates literally to "for this is my blood."[3] However, the copula "to be" (Gk: ἐστιν) by itself does not *require* a literal translation. To understand the meaning of "is" in this context better, we have to turn to the underlying Aramaic and the context of the passage.

The underlying Aramaic that Jesus used at the Last Supper is speculative but largely agreed upon by biblical

---

3 The Greek γάρ (Koine: *gar*; typically not translated or translated "for") is a post-positive which can be used to denote the beginning of a new sentence (but as a post-positive is never placed as the first word of the sentence), or can be understood in a causal way, carrying a meaning similar to "because."

scholars, Catholic and non-Catholic alike. Through an analysis of the Greek text, Jesus likely pronounced the words *dēn biśrî* (literally, "this, my body") and *dēn 'idmî* (literally, "this, my blood") over the bread and wine respectively.[4] The Greek is a faithful translation of this Aramaic wording. While this construction in Aramaic can be interpreted as literal, it does not entirely dismiss the possibility of a figurative understanding of the text.

The context of the Last Supper and the words of Jesus also hint at what Jesus intended to communicate with the words of institution. Jesus uses analogies, similes, and parables when preaching and speaking to His followers, and at times He uses the copula "to be" in a symbolic or representative way. For example, "the harvest is the close of the age, and the reapers are angels" (Mt 13:39), or "I am the light of the world" (Jn 8:12). However, in these contexts, it is made clear in the text that Jesus is talking in parables, "All this Jesus said to the crowds in parables; indeed he said nothing to them without a parable" (Mt 13:34), or He is preaching in an evidently rhetorical setting in which such analogies were commonly used (see Jn 8:12). In the Synoptic Gospels' accounts of the Last Supper, things are different. Jesus's words throughout the entire scene carry a solemn and somber tone. He speaks of a new covenant, of betrayal, and of His death. There is not a single trace of analogy, simile, or parable in the entire chapter. Jesus's words are clear and direct. At the Last Supper, Jesus means what He says and says what He means.

---

4   Ángel Ibáñez, *L'eucaristia, Dono e Mistero: Trattato storico-dogmatico sul mistero eucaristico* (Roma: EDUSC, 2008), 575.

Due to the complications of language, it is impossible to conclude definitively whether Jesus intended the words of institution to be understood solely by analyzing the text. However, based on the Greek text and probable Aramaic words used by Jesus accompanied with the context of the scene and how He utilized and clarified analogies in other passages, an impartial interpretation of the text would conclude that Jesus truly meant the words of institution: "this *really* is my body"; "this *really* is my blood."

"New Covenant"

A new what? Strikingly, all four accounts of the institution of the Eucharist use the exact word "covenant" to describe what kind of blood is in the chalice. To understand what Jesus is communicating to us, we need to understand what a covenant is. God and His people were in a covenant throughout the Old Testament, and God renewed that covenant through many of the Old Testament patriarchs. A sacrifice accompanied each covenant, and each sacrifice provided the blood that ratified the covenant. The blood poured out was like the two parties saying, "I give you my life-blood, my very self, in this covenant," and the sacrificed animal stood as a kind of statement that "I will be like this animal if I break the covenant." For example, Abraham's covenant with God, called the Covenant of the Pieces, included the sacrifice of "a heifer three years old, a she-goat three years old, a ram three years old, a turtledove, and a young pigeon" (Gn 15:9) that Abraham was to cut in two. You can imagine the amount of blood that would have come from cutting that many animals in two.[5] But now, Jesus says that this is a "new covenant in [of] my blood." What does Jesus mean?

The Last Supper is the only time that Jesus says He is establishing a new covenant, so we have to look outside of the Gospels to understand what He means. Hebrews 9:15–20 gives us some direction:

> Therefore he [Jesus] is the mediator of a new covenant, so that those who are called may receive the promised eternal inheritance, since a death has occurred which redeems them from the transgressions under the first covenant. For where a will [covenant][6] is involved, the death of the one who made it must be established. For a will [covenant] takes effect only at death, since it is not in force as long as the one who made it is alive. Hence even the first covenant was not ratified without blood. For when every commandment of the law had been declared by Moses to all the people, he took the blood of calves and goats, with water and scarlet wool and hyssop, and sprinkled both the book itself and all the people, saying, "This is the blood of the covenant which God commanded you."

So, Jesus, who is fully God and fully man, redeemed us from the first covenant by His death. Because Jesus, who is one of the parties of the covenant, had died, the first covenant of the Old Testament ended. To maintain a covenantal relationship with His people, Jesus chose to establish a new covenant on the night before He died. In this new covenant, He would be the sacrifice, and His blood would ratify the covenant. This covenant is different from the first because Jesus died and rose from the dead, never to die again.

---

5   See also the sacrifices in Ex 24:5–8.

6   The Greek word διαθήκη (Koine: *diatheke*) can mean either "will" or "covenant." The NRSVCE2 translation chooses to translate it as "will" in vv. 15–19 and as "covenant" in v. 20, while the original Greek uses the same word throughout.

Therefore, on the part of God, this covenant is eternal. God will never end this covenant. His blood is not just a figure of His lifeblood; it is His lifeblood. The sacrifice that He underwent is not a reminder that one of the parties will die if they break the covenant but that He did die so that the new covenant could not be broken.

What does this have to do with the Real Presence of Christ in the Eucharist? Jesus says that what is in the third cup of the Last Supper is the "blood of the covenant." Hebrews 10:1 establishes that the old covenant was only a shadow of the realities of the new covenant. So, whatever we have in the new covenant must be as real as or more real than what was in the old covenant. In Hebrews 9:19-20, we read that Moses uses real blood to ratify the old covenant. Therefore, the blood of the new covenant cannot be a merely spiritual, symbolic, or intentional presence but rather a Real Presence that was as real as or even more real than the blood sprinkled by Moses. If the chalice of the Last Supper was the blood of the covenant as Jesus declared, then that cup must truly be the blood of Jesus.

"Do This in Remembrance of Me"

This command that appears only in Luke and 1 Corinthians is another vital link to the Catholic Church's teaching on the Real Presence of Christ in the Eucharist. First, it strengthens the argument that the Last Supper was the ritual offering of the sacrifice of the cross, and second, it legitimizes and commands the repetition of this offering.

How does it have anything to do with sacrifice? Following this argument requires some digging and word study

in the Old Testament. The word "to do" was at times used
in the Hebrew Old Testament to mean "to sacrifice." For
example, in Exodus 10:25, Moses explains to Pharaoh,
"You must also let us have sacrifices and burnt offerings,
that we may sacrifice [literally "to do"] to the LORD our
God." The word "to do" is repeatedly used through Exodus 29:35–41 to mean "sacrifice," and in Leviticus 16:24,
the word "to do" is used to describe the offering of the
high priest on the Day of Atonement, "and [he] shall come
forth, and offer his burnt offering and the burnt offering of
the people." Other examples include Numbers 15:11–14,
Judges 13:16, 2 Kings 5:17, Leviticus 9:22, and Ezekiel
43:25. Therefore, when Jesus says to the apostles "do this,"
the saying has sacrificial undertones.

While the saying "do this" isn't enough to solidify a sacrificial understanding of the command, when Jesus follows
with the explanation "in remembrance of me," it becomes
hard to interpret his meaning in other terms. As shown
above, the Passover sacrifice was commanded to be offered
as a memorial, and numerous other sacrifices are referred to
as "remembrances" or "memorials" (cf. Ex 20:24; Lv 2:2;
23:25; 24:7, and many others). Most of these "memorials"
were considered to be sacrifices that reminded God's people of His marvelous works and the covenantal promises
that He made with His people. Likewise, the Mass is the
"memorial sacrifice" that reminds the faithful of Christ's
saving sacrifice and offers the Father the sacrificed body
and blood of the New Lamb of God. The sacrifice of body
and blood offered at the Last Supper, and remembered at
every Mass, is more real than the previous sacrifices that
prefigure it. The previous sacrifices were also made with the

real flesh and blood of the victims offered but, as Hebrews 9 states, the prefigurements are less real than the realities.

The line "do this in remembrance of me" from the Gospels is also crucial for the Real Presence of Christ in the Eucharist today. While these arguments are sufficient for the Real Presence of Christ at the Last Supper, one could argue that they do not apply to the Holy Sacrifice of the Mass today. However, this critical command is the basis for the perpetuation of the sacrifice ritually offered at the Last Supper and consummated on the cross. In fact, Jesus commanded His apostles to "do this," not to "reenact this" or to "pretend like you are doing this." He said to "do this." God never asks us to do what He does not give us the ability to do. Therefore, He also bestowed on the apostles the ability to do what Jesus was doing. That ability, as we will see in the following section, was handed on through the ages to the bishops and priests of Christ's Church.

Conclusion/Review

Key Ideas

- Although there are slight variations in the institution narratives, they substantially use the same wording, and any variations can be dealt with as simple omissions or summaries of longer passages.
- Beginning at the Last Supper, Jesus established the New Covenant and new Passover that would save us from sin and death. Just as the salvation of the old Passover required eating of the flesh of the unblemished lamb, so also the salvation offered by the new Passover sacrifice requires the eating of

the flesh of Jesus, the unblemished Lamb.
- The Greek and probable underlying Aramaic roots of the words of institution suggest no reason for Jesus's words to be taken figuratively. In fact, Jesus seems to be speaking in a very sober and direct manner at that time.
- Jesus established a new covenant through His cross, and the "blood of the covenant" is the chalice at the Last Supper. Since the Old Testament prefigurements used real blood, and the reality is more real than the prefigurement, Jesus's blood of the covenant at the Last Supper must at least be real blood.
- "Do this in remembrance of me" solidifies the sacrificial understanding of the Eucharist and commands the continued offering of the same sacrifice in the Mass by the apostles, bishops, and priests through the ages.

Good Facts and Passages to Memorize

- The institution narratives:
    - Mt 26:26–29
    - Mk 14:22–25
    - Lk 22:14–20
    - 1 Cor 11:23–26
- The institution of the Eucharist is one of the few moments in Christ's life that was recorded four times with almost the exact correspondence of the words and actions in all four accounts. Therefore, the actions and words must have been particularly important to the authors of the

New Testament and the early Church.
- Hebrews 9:15–20 explains the logic of the blood of the covenant.
- "To do" is used throughout the Old Testament to mean "to offer sacrifice."
- "Remembrance" is used throughout the Old Testament to refer to a sacrifice.

Effective Questions to Ask When Discussing the Real Presence

- If the Last Supper and, particularly, the words pronounced over the bread and wine are not constitutive of the saving act of Jesus but rather just a commemorative meal, why is it recorded four times in the New Testament?
- Some argue that Jesus was speaking figuratively at the Last Supper, but is there any textual evidence of this? Or rather, does the textual evidence demonstrate that He was speaking quite literally?
- Some argue that Jesus's "Blood of the Covenant" is not real blood. How can this be if the blood of the sacrifices of the old covenant used real blood and they are only shadows of the fulfillment wrought by Jesus Christ?
- What did Jesus mean when He said, "Do this in remembrance of me"?

3

THE GOSPEL OF JOHN

Introduction

INTERPRETING John 6 is essential to the Catholic understanding of the Real Presence of Christ in the Eucharist and has been debated by non-Catholics from the beginning. Usually, when we discuss this chapter with people who do not believe in the Real Presence, we jump right to the central texts in the bread of life discourse. However, the chapter's entirety is important and is meant to be read as one unit. To make a convincing argument that Jesus meant what He said in the bread of life discourse, we have to recognize what He just finished doing. We also have to accept that the chapter is about more than solely the Eucharist, while not forgetting that the Eucharist holds pride of place in the discourse. To make it easier to study, the whole chapter is listed in the next section, and we'll refer back to it frequently throughout the commentary that follows

The Text: John 6

Feeding the Five Thousand: John 6:1–15

¹ After this Jesus went to the other side of the Sea of Galilee, which is the Sea of Tiberias. ² And a multitude followed him, because they saw the signs which he did on those who were

diseased. [3] Jesus went up into the hills, and there sat down with his disciples. [4] Now the Passover, the feast of the Jews, was at hand. [5] Lifting up his eyes, then, and seeing that a multitude was coming to him, Jesus said to Philip, "How are we to buy bread, so that these people may eat?" [6] This he said to test him, for he knew what he would do. [7] Philip answered him, "Two hundred denarii would not buy enough bread for each of them to get a little." [8] One of his disciples, Andrew, Simon Peter's brother, said to him, [9] "There is a lad here who has five barley loaves and two fish; but what are they among so many?" [10] Jesus said, "Make the people sit down." Now there was much grass in the place; so the men sat down, in number about five thousand. [11] Jesus then took the loaves, and when he had given thanks, he distributed them to those who were seated; so also the fish, as much as they wanted. [12] And when they had eaten their fill, he told his disciples, "Gather up the fragments left over, that nothing may be lost." [13] So they gathered them up and filled twelve baskets with fragments from the five barley loaves, left by those who had eaten. [14] When the people saw the sign that he had done, they said, "This is indeed the prophet who is to come into the world."

[15] Perceiving then that they were about to come and take him by force to make him king, Jesus withdrew again to the hills by himself.

Jesus Walks on the Water: John 6:16–21

[16] When evening came, his disciples went down to the sea, [17] got into a boat, and started across the sea to Capernaum. It was now dark, and Jesus had not yet come to them. [18] The sea rose because a strong wind was blowing. [19] When they had rowed about three or four miles, they saw Jesus walking on the sea and drawing near to the boat. They were frightened, [20] but he said to them, "It is I; do not be afraid." [21] Then they were glad to take him into the boat, and immediately the boat was at the land to which they were going.

The Bread from Heaven: John 6:22–59

[22] On the next day the people who remained on the other side of the sea saw that there had been only one boat there, and that Jesus had not entered the boat with his disciples, but that his disciples had gone away alone. [23] However, boats from Tiberias came near the place where they ate the bread after the Lord had given thanks. [24] So when the people saw that Jesus was not there, nor his disciples, they themselves got into the boats and went to Capernaum seeking Jesus.

[25] When they found him on the other side of the sea, they said to him, "Rabbi, when did you come here?" [26] Jesus answered them, "Truly, I say to you, you seek me, not because you saw signs, but because you ate your fill of the loaves. [27] Do not labor for the food which perishes, but for the food which endures to eternal life, which the Son of Man will give you; for on him has God the Father set his seal." [28] Then they said to him, "What must we do, to be doing the works of God?" [29] Jesus answered them, "This is the work of God, that you believe in him whom he has sent." [30] So they said to him, "Then what sign do you do, that we may see, and believe you? What work do you perform? [31] Our fathers ate the manna in the wilderness; as it is written, 'He gave them bread from heaven to eat.'" [32] Jesus then said to them, "Truly, truly, I say to you, it was not Moses who gave you the bread from heaven; my Father gives you the true bread from heaven. [33] For the bread of God is that which comes down from heaven, and gives life to the world." [34] They said to him, "Lord, give us this bread always."

[35] Jesus said to them, "I am the bread of life; he who comes to me shall not hunger, and he who believes in me shall never thirst. [36] But I said to you that you have seen me and yet do not believe. [37] All that the Father gives me will come to me; and him who comes to me I will not cast out. [38] for I have come down from heaven, not to do my own will, but the will of him who sent me; [39] and this is the will of him who sent me, that I should lose nothing of all that he has given me, but raise it up at the last day. [40] For this is the will of my Father, that every

one who sees the Son and believes in him should have eternal life; and I will raise him up at the last day."

[41] The Jews then murmured at him, because he said, "I am the bread which came down from heaven." [42] They said, "Is not this Jesus, the son of Joseph, whose father and mother we know? How does he now say, 'I have come down from heaven'?" [43] Jesus answered them, "Do not murmur among yourselves. [44] No one can come to me unless the Father who sent me draws him; and I will raise him up at the last day. [45] It is written in the prophets, 'And they shall all be taught by God.' Every one who has heard and learned from the Father comes to me. [46] Not that anyone has seen the Father except him who is from God; he has seen the Father. [47] Truly, truly, I say to you, he who believes has eternal life. [48] I am the bread of life. [49] Your fathers ate the manna in the wilderness, and they died. [50] This is the bread which comes down from heaven, that a man may eat of it and not die. [51] I am the living bread which came down from heaven; if any one eats of this bread, he will live forever; and the bread which I will give for the life of the world is my flesh."

[52] The Jews then disputed among themselves, saying, "How can this man give us his flesh to eat?" [53] So Jesus said to them, "Truly, truly, I say to you, unless you eat the flesh of the Son of Man and drink his blood, you have no life in you; [54] he who eats my flesh and drinks my blood has eternal life, and I will raise him up at the last day. [55] For my flesh is food indeed and my blood is drink indeed. [56] He who eats my flesh and drinks my blood abides in me, and I in him. [57] As the living Father sent me, and I live because of the Father, so he who eats me will live because of me. [58] This is the bread which came down from heaven, not such as the fathers ate and died; he who eats this bread will live for ever." [59] This he said in the synagogue, as he taught at Capernaum.

The Words of Eternal Life: John 6:60–71

⁶⁰ Many of his disciples, when they heard it, said, "This is a hard saying; who can listen to it?" ⁶¹ But Jesus, knowing in himself that his disciples murmured at it, said to them, "Do you take offense at this? ⁶² Then what if you were to see the Son of man ascending where he was before? ⁶³ It is the Spirit that gives life; the flesh is of no avail; the words that I have spoken to you are Spirit and life. ⁶⁴ But there are some of you that do not believe." For Jesus knew from the first who those were that did not believe, and who it was that would betray him. ⁶⁵ And he said, "This is why I told you that no one can come to me unless it is granted by the Father."

⁶⁶ After this many of his disciples turned back and no longer walked with him. ⁶⁷ Jesus said to the twelve, "Will you also go away?" ⁶⁸ Simon Peter answered him, "Lord, to whom shall we go? You have the words of eternal life; ⁶⁹ and we have believed, and have come to know, that you are the Holy One of God." ⁷⁰ Jesus answered them, "Did I not choose you, the Twelve, and one of you is a devil?" ⁷¹ He spoke of Judas the son of Simon Iscariot, for he, one of the twelve, was to betray him.

Commentary on John 6:1–21:
Remember What Comes Before

The first two sections of John 6 are often neglected but are essential to set the scene for the bread of life discourse in John 6:22 and following. In the first scene, Jesus multiplies the loaves and the fishes. The first point to consider is that Jesus chooses to perform a miracle using bread right before He speaks about Himself being the bread of life. This miracle is then referenced again at the beginning of the bread of life discourse (see Jn 6:23, 26). This reference connects it to the discourse and suggests that John intended it to be understood in light of this miracle. Jesus will frequently

join an action or miracle with words, and He uses the action
to emphasize the words and the words to clarify the action
(i.e., healings and forgiveness, walking on water and faith,
etc.). Therefore, Jesus is preparing our understanding for
the bread of life discourse when He speaks about a miracle
involving bread.

The multiplication of the loaves takes on even more
Eucharistic undertones considering it happened when "the
Passover, the feast of the Jews, was near" (Jn 6:4), which
was the same time of the year as the Last Supper. Then, it
becomes even more Eucharistic when Jesus takes the bread.
The text reads, "Jesus then took the loaves, and when he
had given thanks, he distributed them to those who were
seated" (Jn 6:11). The phrase "given thanks" is key. The
Greek word used is εὐχαριστήσας (eucharistesas), from
which the word "Eucharist" comes. In the early Church, the
verb "to give thanks" (eucharistein) was the term used to
mean "celebrate Mass." So while Jesus was not celebrating
Mass at the multiplication of the loaves in John 6, the fact
that John chose to use that wording means that he understood this action to be a prefigurement of the Eucharist and
a preparation for the bread of life discourse.

After the multiplication of the loaves and fishes, Jesus
then performs another miracle, this time in His body. The
disciples get into the boat and begin to cross the sea. A
storm arises and night falls. Jesus walks on the sea after
them and brings them to the other side.

Why did Jesus choose to walk across the water instead
of some other form of transportation? The walking on the
water was not a mere practicality. Jesus chose this. He
could have gotten into the boat with the disciples. He could

have waited until the other boats came to pick Him up. He could have appeared on the other side. Why did He choose to walk on the water? Because He was preparing the disciples for what He was going to say when they arrived at the other shore. Jesus was performing a miracle in His flesh so that the disciples would be ready to accept His teaching that His "flesh is food indeed" (Jn 6:55).

John 6:1–21 are Jesus's preparations for the bread of life discourse. He performs a miracle concerning bread, followed by one involving His flesh. These miracles are meant to prepare the crowd for what He would tell them next: He is the bread come down from heaven, and His flesh is true food.

Commentary on John 6:22–27: It's All Connected

In ancient times, chapters, headings, and subheadings weren't used in writing. A text was just a long string of words and sentences (sometimes even without spaces between the words!) that the reader had to figure out how to divide up. Therefore, when an author wanted to let someone know that two sections of a work were meant to be read in unison, a reference to the previous section(s) was placed at the beginning to connect the two sections and prepare the reader's mind for what comes next.

John 6:22 sets the scene for the bread of life discourse with an allusion to the walking on water and a reference to the multiplication of the loaves: "On the next day the people who remained on the other side of the sea saw that there had been only one boat there, and that Jesus had not entered the boat with his disciples, but that his disciples had gone away alone. However, boats from Tiberias came near the place where they ate the bread after the Lord had given thanks. So when the people saw that Jesus was not there, nor his disciples, they themselves got into the boats and went to Capernaum seeking Jesus" (Jn 6:22–24).[1]

To make it even clearer that the two miracles and the discourse are connected, in the discourse itself, John references each again: "When they found him on the other side of the sea, they said to him, 'Rabbi, when did you come here?' Jesus answered them, 'Truly, truly, I say to you, you seek me, not because you saw signs, but because you ate your fill of the loaves'" (Jn 6:25–26). Therefore, in these first several verses of the discourse, it is as if John is shouting at us, "This is all connected! Read it together! What happened before makes the rest of this believable!"

Commentary on John 6:28–29: Belief

After reminding the reader of these miracles, John then urges us to faith in verse 29: "This is the work of God, that you believe in him whom he has sent." Doing the work of God is making the act of faith in Jesus Christ. John is calling us to make an act of faith before he records Jesus's bread of life discourse. This exhortation is necessary from John's point of view. He clearly remembers how after Jesus explained the Eucharist to them, "many of his disciples turned back and no longer walked with him" (Jn 6:66), so

---

1   There is no reference to the multiplication of loaves mentioned here. It seems that the author considered the multiplication of the fish to be a necessary historical fact but not entirely relevant for what Jesus was intending to teach.

John records the words of Jesus, reinforcing the importance of faith before He begins the discourse.

The connection between the Eucharist and faith has been held from the earliest times. It is evident in the Mass when right after the words of consecration—the words that Jesus used at the Last Supper that transform the bread and wine into the body and blood of Christ—the priest says, "The mystery of faith." The word for "sacrament" in Greek is μυστήριον (*musterion*). Therefore, when the priest sings or says "the mystery of faith," he's saying, "This is the sacrament of faith." The Eucharist is called the sacrament (or mystery) of faith for three reasons:

1. It is the source and summit of our faith, insofar as Jesus is the source and summit of our faith, and the Eucharist is Jesus Christ's body, blood, soul, and divinity really and truly present under the form of bread and wine.

2. If you believe in the Eucharist, you necessarily believe in a whole number of other important teachings: the existence of God, the Trinity, God's power over creation, the sacramental order, apostolic succession, human priesthood, etc.

3. Believing in the Eucharist requires a real act of faith. We see a human being say words over a piece of bread and a chalice of wine that look exactly the same before and after his words. We believe the words of Jesus Christ and know that what was lifeless is now the source of all life, what was powerless is now the All-powerful, and the bread and wine created by human hands is now truly transformed into God, who created us.

Commentary on John 6:30–33: Bread

Jesus's listeners still don't understand. They are fixated on miracles and filling their stomachs. They say to Jesus, "What work do you perform? Our fathers ate the manna in the wilderness" (Jn 6:30–31). Jesus's response clarifies that they are on both the right track and the wrong track: "Truly, truly, I say to you, it was not Moses who gave you the bread from heaven; my Father gives you the true bread from heaven" (Jn 6:32). He reinforces the parallel between Moses giving the manna in the wilderness (see "The Whole Story: The Old Testament Passages" for more information on the manna foreshadowing the Eucharist), but He says that the bread that will come from the Father is the "true bread from heaven." The use of "true" to describe the bread that comes from the Father emphasizes that it is not a symbolic bread, but rather true bread.

Commentary on John 6:34–44: Jesus's Origin

Here comes the transition. Jesus has beautifully set up the idea of the bread from heaven: it endures to eternal life, it requires faith to receive, it comes from the Father, it's the true bread, and it gives life to the world. His listeners are hooked. "Give us this bread always," (Jn 6:34) they say. And then He reveals that: "I am the bread of life" (Jn 6:35). You can imagine the expressions on the faces of His listeners. Some would show surprise, others disgust, others disappointment, but everyone would have been shocked. The next several verses focus on Jesus's origin from the

Father, salvation through Jesus Christ, and the importance of faith in Christ (Jn 6:36–40).

Then the crowd begins to object because He said that He comes from heaven. They knew His supposed father and His mother and did not believe that He could be from heaven. The irony of this scene now becomes striking. The miraculous multiplication of the loaves just fed the crowds, and they had recognized that He was somehow able to travel across the lake without having gotten into a boat. Yet, when He says that He has come down from heaven, they begin to put their foot down. However, Jesus continues to push on. He does not back down in His teaching but instead continues in the same direction, expounding on the importance of faith and the new bread that He will give them.

Commentary on John 6:44–47: Repetition and Reinforcement

From verse 44 to verse 59, Jesus reiterates the same points that He made in verses 25–40: eternal life, the importance of belief, the bread of life, and His origin from the Father. This is particularly important for our topic of the Real Presence of Christ in the Eucharist because, in other passages in John, when the crowds don't understand Him correctly, John records that Jesus later clarifies what He means. In John 6, when the crowds challenge His teachings, John records Jesus speaking in even more forceful terms to clarify.

Verses 44–50 focus on the importance of belief, eternal life, and His origin from the Father. Verse 44 is a kind of compendium of the section: "No one can come to me unless the Father who sent me [Jesus's origin] draws him [the gift of faith]; and I will raise that person up at the last day [eternal life]." Verses 45–46 expound more on Jesus's relationship with the Father.

Verse 47, "Truly, truly, I say to you, he who believes has eternal life," is often used by non-Catholics to derail the point that Jesus is making. They say, "See, this is all about how faith in Jesus saves!" The key here is not to disagree. Jesus is saying that faith saves. But that is just one part of the point He is making in this passage. As in verse 44, this is a compacted version of His argument. The entire argument is that belief is necessary to eat the bread from heaven, and he who eats the bread from heaven has eternal life. So, in verse 47, the middle term "eat the bread from heaven" is skipped to shorten the argument. What is important is that we do not forget that the middle term is still necessary to follow Jesus's argument.

If eating the bread from heaven is necessary to have eternal life, why does Jesus skip over it in verse 47? The answer is that Jesus makes the point clearly in verses 51–58, so it is not necessary to explain everything in verse 47 because He will explain it shortly. The assumption that verse 47 logically includes eating the bread for salvation is the only way to interpret it if one holds that the Bible does not contradict itself (which Catholics and most Christians hold). Verse 53 makes an exclusive claim regarding eating Christ's flesh and blood: "Unless you eat the flesh of the Son of Man and drink his blood, you have no life in you." Therefore, in order to read verse 47 in a way that excludes the Eucharist, you have to interpret verse 53 in a non-literal way (see the next section for why that isn't a reasonable position) or accept that the Bible contradicts itself in the same chapter and only a few verses apart.

Commentary on John 6:48–59: Flesh

Next, Jesus goes even further beyond the crowds' understanding. Not only did He say that He comes from the Father, but He now says that His flesh is the bread that they must eat. Verses 48–50 retrace the topics covered the first time He spoke about the bread from heaven: He is the bread of life; this bread is superior to the manna in the desert; this bread comes down from heaven; this bread gives eternal life. Then He said what was most appalling to the Jews: "The bread which I will give for the life of the world is my flesh" (Jn 6:51).

The crowd understood Him to be speaking literally, but the content of His teaching was too shocking for them to accept: "How can this man give us his flesh to eat?" (Jn 6:52). Instead of backing down by clarifying His words as He would have when explaining one of His parables, or by assuring them that He was using an analogy, Jesus instead says it even more clearly: "Truly, truly, I say to you, unless you eat the flesh of the Son of Man and drink his blood, you have no life in you; he who eats my flesh and drinks my blood has eternal life, and I will raise him up at the last day. For my flesh is food indeed and my blood is drink indeed" (Jn 6:53–55).

Those words are the core of the message in John chapter 6: eating Jesus's flesh brings eternal life. At this passage, anyone who does not believe in the Real Presence of Christ in the Eucharist is forced to interpret these words

in a non-literal way. In response to those who only interpret the passage figuratively, it is worth asking if Jesus had
wanted to communicate that His flesh was true food and
His blood was true drink, how else would He have said it?
He has already explained that the true bread comes down
from heaven, He who eats this bread will have eternal life,
and His flesh is the bread. Is there a more forceful and convincing way of saying it? He starts with the words "Truly,
truly" (literally, "Amen, amen"), which is a way of saying, "this is important, so listen to me." Then He makes
the exclusive statement about having to eat His flesh and
drink His blood in order to have life without any reference
to bread so that we don't get confused. Next, in case we
thought He was talking about natural life, He clarifies that
eating His flesh and drinking His blood cause eternal life
and the resurrection on the last day.

The translation used in this work inadequately conveys
perhaps the most lucid statement: "my flesh is food indeed
and my blood is drink indeed" (Jn 6:53–55). What the version translates as "is food indeed" and "is drink indeed"
in Greek is ἀληθής ἐστι βρῶσις (koine: *Alethes esti bro-
sis*) and ἀληθής ἐστι πόσις (koine: *Alethes esti posis*).
The Greek word ἀληθής, which this version translates as
"indeed," literally means "true." Therefore, a closer translation is "true food" and "true drink." This repetition of
"true" makes it clear that Jesus is talking about the actual
eating and drinking of real food.

If we ignore the forcefulness and the clarity of the words
of Jesus and choose to interpret Him figuratively or anal-
ogously, there are serious problems. When interpreting
a historical text like the Bible, we have to read it in the

context in which it was written. Certain phrases or sayings could have meant one thing at that time, whereas they can mean nothing or something completely different today. Eating the flesh of someone and drinking their blood is one of those sayings. In the Hebrew-Aramaic linguistic environment at the time of Jesus, to "eat someone's flesh" or to "drink someone's blood" was a figure of speech that meant to persecute and assault the person. For example, we read in Psalm 27:2, "When evildoers assail me to devour my flesh—my adversaries and foes—they shall stumble and fall" (see also Is 9:18–20; Mi 3:3; Rv 17:6, 16). Therefore, if we want to choose to read this passage figuratively, the historically authentic interpretation would be that Jesus is saying to His disciples that only people who persecute and assault Jesus can have eternal life. However, that is contrary to the teachings of Christ (see Mt 26:24; Jn 13:34; Jn 15:15; Lk 10:27). Therefore, in order to accept a non-literal interpretation of this passage, one has to admit that Jesus is teaching us that we cannot have eternal life if we do not persecute and assault Him, or one has to ignore the ordinary figurative meaning of eating someone's flesh at the historical time of Jesus.

The use of the term "true" in verse 55 to describe the food and drink is why the Catholic Church uses the word "real" to describe the presence of Christ in the Eucharist. Logically, what is true is what is real, and what is real is what is true. Therefore, the two terms are almost interchangeable. In Latin, which is the language the Church uses to define her teachings, the word *vere* can mean both "true" and "real" depending on the context, which is why we refer to Jesus's presence in the Eucharist as both a "true presence" and "real presence."

Based on the use of "true" in verse 55, Christ's flesh and blood are really and truly present in the Eucharist. This understanding excludes any of the other lesser presences proposed throughout history. It's not just a "spiritual presence"; it's not just a "dynamic presence"; it's not just a "presence in power"; it's a "true and real presence." Jesus is also present in the Eucharist in a spiritual, dynamic, and powerful way, but if by using those descriptions one means that He is not as really and truly present as He was in the manger, in the home at Nazareth, as He walked the shores of the Sea of Galilee, as He hung on the cross, and as He appeared in the upper room after the Resurrection, then they limit what the Scriptures are saying.

Commentary on John 6:60–71: A Hard Saying

This section of John 6 starts with the disciples having a hard time understanding Jesus. They approach Him and ask, "This is a hard saying; who can listen to it?" (Jn 6:60). This is Jesus's last chance to explain what He meant, and He doesn't back down.

People misunderstand Jesus at several other points in John's Gospel, but every time that happens, John clarifies what Jesus meant. In John 2:19–21, Jesus says that He will rebuild "this temple" in three days. The Jews thought He was talking about the temple in Jerusalem, but John clarifies that "he was speaking of the temple of his body" (v. 21). In John 3:3–5, Jesus says that "unless one is born anew, he cannot see the kingdom of God." Nicodemus understands

Him to be speaking of physical birth, but Jesus clarifies in verse 5 that He is speaking of a rebirth "of water and Spirit" (i.e., Baptism). In John 4:11–12, the Samaritan woman thinks that Jesus is talking about physical water, but He then reveals to her that He is the Messiah. In John 4:31–34, the disciples think that Jesus is talking about literal food, but He then clarifies that "my food is to do the will of him who sent me" (v. 34). In John 8:32–34, Jesus says that the truth will make you free. The Jews understand Him to be speaking of physical slavery, but He clarifies that "every one who commits sin is a slave to sin" (v. 34). Why is it that Jesus doesn't correct them this time? The only reasonable answer is because they understood Him correctly: His flesh is true food, and His blood is true drink.

Verse 63, "It is the spirit that gives life; the flesh is of no avail," is a favorite go-to verse for those who want to read John chapter 6 in a symbolic way. They say, "If the flesh is of no avail, why would Jesus make us eat His flesh? It can't truly be His flesh!" But there is a glaring issue with their argument: to claim that the flesh is of no avail is to claim that Jesus is of no avail. The Word of God took flesh (Jn 1; 1 Jn 4:2), and in the flesh, He died on the cross to pay the debt of our sins and redeem us (1 Pt 3:18), and then in the flesh, He rose from the dead to give us eternal life (Jn 20:24–29). All of Jesus's actions in the flesh are core elements of salvation, so if we read verse 63 literally, then we would incorrectly conclude that His salvific work is useless.

Others will approach verse 63 claiming that Jesus is clarifying that His previous sayings are to be read symbolically, not literally. They claim that the "spirit" means "symbolic"

interpretation and the "flesh" means "literal" interpretation. However, nowhere in the Scriptures is "spirit" used
to indicate a figurative interpretation. Therefore, that argument has no real backing in the Scriptures. A much more
reasonable interpretation of verse 63 is to understand the
dichotomy between the spirit and the flesh as referring
to the spiritual and carnal men who do the works of the
spirit and the works of the flesh, respectively.[2] Finally, St.
Augustine, the fourth-century bishop and theologian, sums
up the proper interpretation with these words:

> So what is it that he adds: "The Spirit gives life, the flesh
> profits nothing"? Let's say to Him (for he allows it if we are
> desiring to know and not to contradict him): O Lord, good
> teacher, how can "the flesh profit nothing", if you said:
> "Unless you eat my flesh, and drink my blood, you shall not
> have life"? Does life profit nothing? And what is our purpose
> if not that we may have eternal life which you promise by
> your flesh? What do you mean by "the flesh profits nothing"?
> It does profit nothing, but in the way they understood it: for
> they understood the flesh as cut out from a corpse or sold in
> the meat market, not as alive with a spirit. That is why it is
> said. "the flesh profits nothing"; in the same way it is said,
> "knowledge puffs up". . . . For if the flesh profited nothing, the
> Word would not have become flesh, that he might dwell among
> us. If through the flesh, Christ profited us greatly, how does
> the flesh profit nothing? Through the flesh the Spirit worked
> for our salvation. The flesh was a vessel; pay attention to what
> it held, not what it was. The Apostles were sent forth; did their
> flesh profit us nothing? If the flesh of the Apostles profited
> us, can the flesh of the Lord profit us nothing? For, how does
> the sound of words reach us, if not through the voice of the
> flesh? How can the pen move, or how does writing happen?
> All these things are the work of flesh, but moved by the spirit

---

2   To read more about the theology of the spirit and the flesh, see 1 Cor
     2:14–3:4 and Gal 5:16–26, where Paul develops this theology well.

as its instrument. "The spirit gives life, but the flesh profits nothing" is in regard to how they understood flesh, which is not how I give my flesh to eat.[3]

Verse 66 is another important text to support the Church's teaching on the Real Presence of Christ in the Eucharist. It reads, "After this many of his disciples turned back and no longer walked with him." Why did they turn back? Remember, it was His *disciples* that no longer walked with Him. The disciples were not the people passing by who happened to listen. They were not the people who were just hoping to see the next miracle or get the next free meal. The disciples were the ones who were committed to following the teachings of Jesus. If Jesus was simply teaching that belief in Him is necessary for salvation, why did *many* disciples walk away? If Jesus was just saying that He was the figurative bread from heaven, why did His *disciples* turn back? What is so shocking about either of those interpretations to make the disciples no longer walk with Him? Nothing. They turned away because He told them that they had to eat His flesh and drink His blood to have eternal life. That is a hard saying.

Some things have remained the same since the time of Jesus. There are still many people today who reject Jesus's teaching on His Real Presence in the Eucharist. There are many who walk away because this teaching is just too hard to believe. John was aware of the difficulty in his time, which is why he prepared us by recounting the miracle with bread—the multiplication of the loaves—and the miracle with Jesus's flesh—walking on the water—before presenting the bread of life discourse. Even within the bread of life

3   Augustine, *Tractatus In Jo. 27, 5*, PL 35, 1617–1618.

discourse, Jesus urges us to make the act of faith in Him because the Father sent Him. It is because Jesus came from the Father that we can have faith in His words, "My flesh is food indeed and my blood is drink indeed" (Jn 6:55), "This is my body" (Mt 26:26; Mk 14:22; Lk 22:19; 1 Cor 11:24), and "This is my blood" (Mt 26:29; Mk 14:24; Cf. Lk 22:20; 1 Cor 11:25).

Conclusion/Review

Key Ideas

- John 6 is the longest and most developed passage in the New Testament concerning the Eucharist.
- John 6 is meant to be read as one unit made up of the multiplication of the loaves, the walking on the water, and the bread of life discourse. The miracles prepare the reader's faith for the strong statement that Jesus makes in the discourse.
- The bread of life discourse is principally about the Eucharist, but it is not exclusively about the Eucharist. It also talks about Jesus's relationship with the Father and the gift of faith.
- Any interpretation other than the one that holds that Jesus was speaking literally requires making claims that cannot be substantiated elsewhere in the Scriptures or that contradict something else Jesus explicitly taught.

Good Facts and Passages to Memorize

- The bread of life discourse is intentionally preceded by the miracle of the multiplication of the loaves and of the walking on the water to prepare the reader's mind to accept the miracle of the Eucharist that Jesus expounds upon in the discourse.

- John 6:48: "I am the bread of life."
- John 6:53–55: "Truly, truly, I say to you, unless you eat the flesh of the Son of Man and drink his blood, you have no life in you; he who eats my flesh and drinks my blood have eternal life, and I will raise him up at the last day. For my flesh is [true] food indeed and my blood is [true] drink indeed."
- As St. Augustine teaches, verse 63 ("It is the spirit that gives life; the flesh is of no avail") is saying that eating dead flesh (i.e., cannibalism) is useless. Jesus is saying that His flesh gives life and, therefore, is not dead flesh.

Effective Questions to Ask When Discussing the Real Presence

- If Jesus was just talking about how faith in Him is necessary for salvation, why did so many of His disciples walk away? Why was that such a hard saying?
- If you were Jesus and wanted to teach that your flesh was true food and your blood was true drink, how would you say it more forcefully and convincingly than Jesus does in John 6:53–55?
- If Jesus didn't mean that His flesh was really intended to be eaten and His blood wasn't really intended to be drunk, why did He not back down at any of the three times that He was questioned?

4

AFTER THE CRUCIFIXION

Introduction

THE Bible doesn't stop its references to the Eucharist at the death of Christ. The authors wanted to make it clear that the Eucharist was meant to continue throughout the Church's life. We see the risen Jesus, the apostles, and the early Church leaders celebrate the Eucharist at different points throughout the New Testament. These passages are important to the topic of the Real Presence of Christ in the Eucharist because they show that the early Church gave centrality to the earthshattering claim that Jesus took the form of bread and wine.[1] First Corinthians further develops and explains the theology of the Eucharist as it is applied in the life of the nascent Church. These passages help us to understand that the early Church not only celebrated "the breaking of the bread" but also reflected on what it was doing, was concerned to correct abuses, and considered it central to the saving act of Christ.

---

1   See the introduction to chapter 1 for more of an explanation on the significance of these references to the overall argument.

The Road to Emmaus

Luke 24 is a well-known Scripture passage for many reasons. Specifically, it is the first record of the celebration of the Eucharist after the Resurrection. Here is the text:

> That very day two of them were going to a village called Emmaus, about seven miles from Jerusalem, and talking with each other about all these things that had happened. While they were talking and discussing together, Jesus himself drew near and went with them. But their eyes were kept from recognizing him. And he said to them, "What is this conversation which you are holding with each other as you walk?" They stood still, looking sad. Then one of them, named Cleopas, answered him, "Are you the only visitor to Jerusalem who does not know the things that have happened there in these days?" And he said to them, "What things?" And they said to him, "Concerning Jesus of Nazareth, who was a prophet mighty in deed and word before God and all the people, and how our chief priests and rulers delivered him up to be condemned to death and crucified him. But we had hoped that he was the one to redeem Israel. Yes, and besides all this, it is now the third day since this happened. Moreover, some women of our company amazed us. They were at the tomb early in the morning, and did not find his body; and they came back saying that they had even seen a vision of angels, who said that he was alive. Some of those who were with us went to the tomb and found it just as the women had said; but him they did not see." And he said to them, "Oh foolish men, and slow of heart to believe all that the prophets have spoken! Was it not necessary that the Christ should suffer these things and enter into his glory?" And beginning with Moses and all the prophets, he interpreted to them in all the Scriptures the things concerning himself.
>
> So they drew near to the village to which they were going. He appeared to be going further, but they constrained him, saying, "Stay with us, for it is almost evening and the day is now far spent." So he went in to stay with them. When he was

at the table with them, he took the bread and blessed and broke it, and gave it to them. And their eyes were opened and they recognized him; and he vanished out of their sight. They said to each other, "Did not our hearts burn within us while he talked to us on the road, while he opened to us the Scriptures?" And they rose that same hour and returned to Jerusalem; and they found the eleven gathered together and those who were with them, who said, "The Lord has risen indeed, and has appeared to Simon!" Then they told what had happened on the road, and how he was known to them in the breaking of the bread. (Lk 24:13–35)

There are two small details to note before going into a more in-depth commentary on the portion of the text that focuses on the Eucharist: Firstly, the walk to Emmaus happened the "very day" of the Resurrection. Jesus lost no time in celebrating the Eucharist with His disciples. Also, that means this day was a Sunday, which was the day on which the early Church celebrated the Eucharist. Therefore, this passage is a literary unit that says, "The Lord was the first one to teach us to celebrate the Eucharist after His death, and He chose to do it on a Sunday." Secondly, the whole passage has a two-part structure that mimics the structure of the early Christians' Eucharistic celebrations: there is a focus and explanation on the law, prophets, and life of Jesus. Today, this has been preserved in the Liturgy of the Word. Then there is the consecration and reception of the Eucharist, which today is called the Liturgy of the Eucharist. Therefore, the whole passage develops as if it were one long traveling Mass.

It's reasonable to ask where this passage mentions the Eucharist. At first glance, it is not exceedingly clear, but if one understands the vocabulary that the early Christians used to talk about the Eucharist, it stands out clearly. First, there is a set of verbs used in the early Church to describe the action of celebrating the Eucharist: take, bless (or give thanks), break, and give. All of the Last Supper accounts in the Gospels use these words to describe the actions of Jesus in the upper room (see Mt 26:26; Mk 14:22; Lk 22:19). In Luke 24:30, those exact verbs are used: "When he was at the table with them, he took the bread and blessed and broke it, and gave it to them."

Next, an even more precise term for the Eucharist is used to describe what Jesus did with the disciples: the breaking of the bread. "Breaking bread" at the time of Jesus could denote a community meal without any religious significance. Within the Jewish religious context, "breaking bread" was used as a common term for the host's action to initiate others into one of the meal-prayer rituals of the Jewish people. However, through the first years of Christianity, the phrase "the breaking of the bread" became a very precise term for celebrating the Supper of the Lord.

Luke 24:35 is difficult to understand if the phrase "breaking bread" is not interpreted in this way. Suppose we consider "breaking of bread" to mean a common meal. Why is it that Jesus disappeared right when they took the bread? That seems like an impolite gesture for a dinner guest, let alone God Himself. Also, why did Jesus's disappearance during dinner suddenly open their eyes? And if it was Jesus's disappearance that opened their eyes, why did they run all the way back to the apostles to tell them that Jesus "was known to them in the breaking of the bread" (Lk 24:35)? Why didn't they say that He was made known to them in the disappearing act? If it was all about having a meal with Jesus, why doesn't it say He was made known to them *at* the breaking of the bread instead of *in* the breaking of the bread? If we hold that the "breaking of the bread" was a common meal, the rest of the passage simply doesn't make sense.

If we interpret "breaking of the bread" to mean "a Jewish meal-prayer ritual," we're getting closer, but it still doesn't make sense. The new sacrifice of Jesus on the cross has been consummated. The Old Law has given way to the New. Why is Jesus using old covenant rituals? Also, why does Jesus disappear in the middle of a prayer ritual? Once again, this interpretation remains unclear.

If we accept that this "breaking of the bread" was a celebration of the Eucharist, the rest of the passage comes together. Why does it say that Jesus "vanished from their sight" as opposed to "went away"? Because with His Real Eucharistic Presence before them, they did not need His resurrected fleshly presence. He was still there; they just couldn't see His body, only the appearances of bread and wine as we do today. Why do they say that He was made known to them "*in* (gk. ἐν; *en*) the breaking of the bread" as opposed to "*at* (gk. ἐπὶ; *epi*) the breaking of the bread"? Because they recognized Him present in the external appearances of the bread, not because He was breaking the bread in an ordinary way. The passage simply makes sense when we accept that Jesus celebrated the Eucharist with the disciples in Emmaus.

Acts of the Apostles

The phrase "breaking bread" is also used in the Acts of the Apostles to mean celebrating the Eucharist. This usage reinforces the interpretation given above of Luke 24 because Luke is the author of both the Gospel of Luke and the Acts of the Apostles, and he wrote the two to be read in light of each other. If Luke used "breaking of bread" to mean something more than an ordinary meal in one of the books, then it's likely that he did so in the other as well. The first instance of that use is in Acts 2:42–46: "And they held steadfastly to the apostles' teaching and fellowship, to the breaking of bread and to the prayers. And fear upon every soul; and many wonders and signs were done through the apostles. And all who believed were together and had all things in common; they sold their possessions and goods and distributed them to all, as any had need. And day by day, attending the temple together and breaking bread in their homes, they partook of food with glad and generous hearts."

This text depicts the life of the nascent Church. It says they *held steadfastly* to four things: the apostles' teaching, fellowship (better translated as "communal life"), breaking of bread, and the prayers. If we interpret "breaking of bread" as merely a meal, why did eating dinner make it into the list with elements as important as the apostles' teaching, the communal life, and prayers? Also, why did Luke find it necessary to list eating as something that the early Church "held steadfastly" to? The early Church grew quickly, but that is in reference to numbers, not weight. Once again, this interpretation does not make sense. But if we interpret "breaking of bread" to mean the Supper of the Lord, it fits in perfectly. If Jesus is present in the Eucharist, it makes absolute sense that the early Church held steadfastly to the Eucharist.

Some might object: "But it says in verse 46 that they broke bread at home. You eat dinner at home; therefore, it must be a reference to a regular meal." This argument forgets one of the major points of early Christianity: the larger religious institutions did not accept Christians at the time. They could not celebrate the Eucharist in the temple or the synagogues, so they followed the example of Jesus and celebrated the Eucharist in someone's house. The same argument can be made here as above: If they are referring to eating a common meal in this verse, why is it paralleled with spending much time in the temple? It would once again be an odd detail to include in such a setting: "They spent lots of time praying and preaching, but they never packed a lunch. They always ate at home, and that made them happy." Thanks for the detail, but why tell us that now? It must be because this is not an ordinary meal with ordinary food. This passage is talking about the bread of life.

The next reference to celebrating the breaking of the bread in Acts is chapter 20, verses 7 and 10. Here are the verses in context:

> On the first day of the week, when we were gathered together to break bread, Paul talked with them, intending to depart the next day; and he prolonged his speech until midnight. There were many lights in the upper chamber where we were gathered. A young man named Eutychus was sitting in the window. He sank into a deep sleep as Paul talked still longer; and being overcome by sleep, he fell down from the third story and was taken up dead. But Paul went down and bent over him, and embracing him said, "Do not be alarmed, for his life is in him." And when Paul had gone up and had broken bread and eaten, he conversed with them a long while, until

daybreak, and so departed. And they took the lad away alive, and were not a little comforted. (Acts 20:7–12)

Like the Road to Emmaus, this scene happens on Sunday, "the first day of the week" (Acts 20:7). There is another important nugget: "when we were gathered together to break bread" (Acts 20:7). Luke is clarifying that Sunday is the day in which the first Christians ordinarily celebrated this special breaking of bread, and it can be understood that the breaking of the bread was the purpose of the gathering. Also, this scene follows the structure of the Eucharistic gatherings throughout the history of the Church. The first portion, centered on the Scriptures, includes a homily (note that Paul preaches for so long that someone falls asleep and falls out the window!), followed by the second portion centered on the consecration and reception of the Eucharist. Notice that the celebration was also held in an upper room on the third story of a house. These details make it clear that Paul's actions were what the early Church Fathers described as the Eucharist. This shows that there is a clear continuity between the life of Jesus, the life of the nascent Church in the Acts of the Apostles, and the early Church in celebrating the Supper of the Lord.

The last reference to the breaking of bread occurs in Acts 27:

As it was about to dawn, Paul urged them all to take some food, saying, "Today is the fourteenth day that you have continued in suspense and without food, having taken nothing. Therefore I urge you to take some food; it will give you strength, since not a hair is to perish from the head of any of you." And when he had said this, he took bread, and giving thanks to God in the presence of all, he broke it and began to eat. Then they all were encouraged and ate some food themselves. (We were in all two hundred and seventy-six persons in the ship.) And when they had eaten enough, they lightened the ship, throwing the wheat into the sea. (Acts 27:33–38)

Here we see the use of the four verbs (take, give thanks/ bless, break, give) that describe the liturgical action of celebrating the Eucharist, with one slight modification. This time, Paul takes the bread, gives thanks, and breaks the bread, but doesn't give it to anyone. He simply begins to eat. Why? The answer is in the context. He was on a ship with sailors, soldiers, and prisoners. There is a fairly low chance that any of them would have been professed and baptized Christians. Therefore, keeping in mind that the Eucharist was not given to non-believers,[2] it makes sense that Paul didn't "give" his food to anyone else because there was something sacred about the food that he was eating. Instead, the passage says, "Then they all were encouraged and ate some food themselves" (Acts 27:36). This exclusive consumption of the food, along with the breaking of bread and giving thanks,[3] make it clear that Paul celebrated the Eucharist in this passage as well.

First Corinthians

The rich theology of the Eucharist that was developed in the first years of the Church is also seen in Paul's dealing with the controversies of the Church in Corinth. 1 Corinthians 10:14–22 is the central passage:

Therefore, my beloved, shun the worship of idols. I speak as to sensible men; judge for yourselves what I say. The cup of

2　See chapter 7 on St. Justin Martyr.
3　We derive the word "Eucharist" from the Greek word "to give thanks."

blessing which we bless, is it not a participation in the blood of
Christ? The bread which we break, is it not a participation in the
body of Christ? Because there is one bread, we who are many
are one body, for we all partake of the one bread. Consider the
people of Israel; are not those who eat the sacrifices partners
in the altar? What do I imply then? That food offered to idols
is anything, or that an idol is anything? No, I imply that what
pagans sacrifice they offer to demons and not to God. I do not
want you to be partners with demons. You cannot drink the
cup of the Lord and the cup of demons. You cannot partake
of the table of the Lord and the table of demons. Shall we
provoke the Lord to jealousy? Are we stronger than he?

The passage occurs within a discussion of the eating of
meat that had previously been sacrificed to idols. Paul
clarifies that there is no problem with the meat per se but
with the possibility of being seen as worshiping idols. If
they know the meat has been sacrificed to idols, then they
should not eat the meat to avoid confusing other people:
"But if someone says to you, 'This has been offered in sacrifice,' then out of consideration for the man who informed
you, and for conscience' sake—I mean his conscience, not
yours—do not eat it" (1 Cor 10:28–29). Christians should
never do something that could be seen as worshiping an
idol, because idol worship, which Paul calls "sacrifice
to demons" (1 Cor 10:20), is completely contrary to the
Christian life.

Paul's argument for why worshiping idols is unaccept-
able is rooted in the Eucharist: "The cup of blessing which
we bless, is it not a participation in the blood of Christ?
The bread which we break, is it not a participation in the
body of Christ?" (1 Cor 10:16). There are a few interesting
points to consider with these rhetorical questions: Firstly,

they are rhetorical questions with the phrase "is it not," which is used when everyone agrees with the fundamental assumption: that the cup of blessing and bread we break is a sharing in the blood and body of Christ. Therefore, this was a commonly held teaching. It was not some new teaching of Paul but rather something that all Christians held from the earliest times. Secondly, Paul refers to the cup as "the cup of blessing," which is the third cup's name in the Passover ritual. This use of "cup of blessing" reinforces the link between the Passover and the Eucharist as described above in chapters 1 and 2 of this book.

The central point of the argument is found in the parallel of verse 21: "You cannot drink the cup of the Lord and the cup of demons. You cannot partake of the table of the Lord and the table of demons." Paul sets up a comparison that implies a similarity and opposition between flesh and blood offered to idols and the flesh and blood of Christ in the Eucharist. They can be compared because each contains real body and blood offered in sacrifice, but they are diametrically opposed because of the person to whom they are offered. It is also striking that Paul was previously only speaking of eating meat offered to idols, but he includes drinking the cup when he introduces this parallel. Why? Because when the Christians celebrated the Supper of the Lord, they always offered both the bread and the cup. Therefore, in the early Christians' minds, a cup of demons had to be inserted for the comparison to be complete.

Chapter 11 of the First Letter to the Corinthians holds good evidence of a theological reflection on the Eucharist as well:

> Whoever, therefore, eats the bread or drinks the cup of the
> Lord in an unworthy manner will be guilty of profaning for
> the body and blood of the Lord. Let a man examine himself,
> and so eat of the bread and drink of the cup. For any one who
> eats and drinks without discerning the body eats and drinks
> judgment upon himself. That is why many of you are weak
> and ill, and some have died. But if we judged ourselves truly,
> we should not be judged. But when we are judged by the Lord,
> we are chastened so that we may not be condemned along
> with the world.
>
> So then, my brethren, when you come together to eat,
> wait for one another—if any one is hungry, let him eat at
> home—lest when you come together to be condemned. (1 Cor
> 11:27–34)

This passage immediately follows Paul's institution narrative.[4] Before exploring the first portion, it's worth briefly
looking at the end of the quotation because it clarifies that
this is not an ordinary meal. Paul says, "If any one is hungry, let him eat at home—lest when you come together to
be condemned" (1 Cor 11:34). This passage sits within
Paul's reprimand of the Corinthians for their unworthy
celebration of the Lord's Supper. One issue is that some
Corinthians are bringing so much food that they are even
becoming drunk, while others go hungry: "For in eating,
each one goes ahead with his own meal, and one is hungry and another is drunk. What! Do you not have houses
to eat and drink in?" (1 Cor 11:21–22). If this were an
ordinary meal, Paul would not have told them to eat at
home but rather to share. Instead, he reprimands them for
approaching the Eucharist as an ordinary meal and not truly
as the Lord's Supper: "When you meet together, is it not
the Lord's supper that you eat" (1 Cor 11:20). Therefore,

---

4   See chapter 2 of this book.

Paul's understanding of the Lord's Supper is not that of an ordinary meal but rather as something unique that Christians do when gathered together.

With a proper understanding of the context, we can now consider Paul's reprimand. Paul makes a powerful statement, "Whoever, therefore, eats the bread or drinks the cup of the Lord in an unworthy manner will be guilty of profaning the body and blood of the Lord" (1 Cor 11:27). To "be guilty of profaning (the Greek ἔνοχος, *enochos* literally means just "guilty") the body and blood of the Lord" is homicidal language. The phrase "guilty of blood" means that one is responsible for the murder of someone. For example, at the trial of Jesus, Pilate washes his hands and says, "I am innocent of this man's blood; see to it yourselves" (Mt 24:27), meaning "I am not guilty of this man's murder."

If Jesus were not truly present in the Eucharist, this would be an odd statement by Paul. Why is someone guilty of murder if they unworthily receive something that is just a representation of the body and blood of Christ? Also, why is it that "anyone who eats and drinks without discerning the body, eats and drinks judgment upon himself" (1 Cor 11:29)? If it is bread, why are there such grave consequences to eating it unworthily? The most reasonable response is because it really is Jesus's body and blood as understood within the institution narrative's context that precedes this passage.

Conclusion/Review

Key Ideas

- The Church's teaching on the Eucharist does not rely exclusively on the Gospels; rather, her teachings are based on the entire New Testament.
- Luke, in the passage on the road to Emmaus, records Jesus celebrating the Eucharist after the Resurrection, and Acts says that the first Christians dedicated themselves to the celebration of the Eucharist.
- In the First Letter to the Corinthians, Paul continues to develop a theology of the Eucharist, and he considers the Eucharist important enough to merit correcting certain abuses in the Church in Corinth.

Good Facts and Passages to Memorize

- Luke 24:13–25: The road to Emmaus was on the Sunday of the Resurrection, follows the Mass's structure, and Jesus in His resurrected body "vanished out of their sight" at the moment of the consecration because they recognized Him in the Eucharist.
- Two phrases used to describe the celebration of the Eucharist in the early Church are the four verbs "take", "bless" (or give thanks), "break," and "give" and the shorter version "break bread."
- Acts 2:42: "They held steadfastly to the apostles' teaching and fellowship, to the breaking of the bread and to the prayers."

- Paul celebrated the Eucharist in Acts 20:7–11 (when Eutychus falls out the window) and Acts 27:35 (before the shipwreck).
- 1 Corinthians 10 and 11 contain Paul's theological reflection on the Eucharist and his correction of the Corinthians for not celebrating it worthily.

Effective Questions to Ask When Discussing the Real Presence

- In Emmaus, why does Jesus vanish from their sight right after breaking the bread?
- Some argue that the "breaking of bread" signifies just a regular meal. If that were the case, why would St. Paul state that the early Christians "dedicated themselves" to it?
- If Jesus isn't really present in the Eucharist, why does Paul say that whoever eats it unworthily is guilty of profaning the body and blood of the Lord?
- If the bread and wine used in the Lord's Supper do not truly become the body and blood of Jesus, why do those who do not recognize His body and blood in the Eucharist eat and drink judgment against themselves? Are they being condemned for discerning the truth?

PART II

WHAT DO THE FATHERS SAY?

A S shown in the previous section, when the Bible is read with all of the texts in mind, it teaches clearly that the Eucharist is the true flesh and blood of Christ. Nevertheless, many people today have chosen to interpret figuratively all of the passages that address the Real Presence of Christ in the Eucharist. By reading passages in an isolated manner—and not in the light of the rest of the Scriptures—they are doubtful about which interpretation is correct. They are unable to accept the bold claim that a host that looks like bread is actually Jesus Himself. Instead they choose to believe that Jesus is only present in power, spirit, or symbol.

At the center of the disagreement is the question of which interpretation of the Bible is correct. When looking at each of the texts in an isolated way, any level-headed interpreter of the Scriptures would say, "Without any context, we could understand this passage in several different ways." Arguing in circles about the proper interpretation two thousand years after the text was written is futile. So, as Catholics, we turn to the early Church Fathers—the saints and leaders of the first several hundred years of Christianity—and ask what the first Christians believed.

The Fathers of the Church are reliable for a few different
reasons:

1. They were the disciples of the apostles (or the
   disciples of the apostles' disciples). As Catholics, we believe that the Holy Spirit preserves
   the teachings of Jesus in the Church throughout
   history. However, even for someone who doesn't
   believe that the Holy Spirit guides the Church's
   teaching, they are reliable because of their proximity to Jesus. In ancient times, the discipleship
   system was one in which the disciple's duty was
   to internalize the teachings and way of life of
   the master completely. Eventually, the disciple
   became a master, and then his duty was to hand
   on accurately the teachings and way of life of his
   master. Therefore, even if the Holy Spirit didn't
   guide the Church, it's reasonable that they would
   have accurately preserved Jesus's teachings for at
   least several generations of disciples.
2. They gave us the New Testament. The New
   Testament was written in apostolic times, which
   means that it was written during the era of the
   apostles' lifetimes. However, it wasn't compiled
   as a clearly defined set of inspired texts until the
   third or fourth century. There are many writings
   from apostolic times, but not all of them were
   included in the Bible. Who chose which books
   belong in the Bible? The early Christians. The
   Holy Spirit guided them to select and preserve
   the books that He had inspired as Holy Scripture. By trusting the early Christians to tell us

which books are inspired, it's reasonable to trust them to tell us *what* those books are telling us.

3. They were holy people. Today, we put more credence in the teachings of Christians who live holy lives. These Fathers of the Church were the great saints of their time. They lived heroic holiness and often gave their lives as martyrs of Jesus Christ. On a human level, they are reliable because their teachings are coherent with their way of life. As Christians, we also know that the Holy Spirit is the Spirit of Truth, so when we see many people who are living heroic holiness and who are teaching the same thing, it is a good sign that they teach the truth.

With the Fathers of the Church as our guide in interpreting the Scriptures, we are going to see a few things: a) all of the teachings of the Church Fathers are compatible with the Catholic Church's teaching on the Real Presence of Christ in the Eucharist; b) some of the teachings of the Church Fathers can only be interpreted to coincide with the Real Presence of Christ in the Eucharist; c) despite the Fathers of the Church continually calling out heresy and ferociously fighting to eradicate it, not one Father of the Church ever disputes or attacks someone who teaches the Real Presence of Christ in the Eucharist.

What the Church Teaches

Before trying to prove the Real Presence of Christ in the Eucharist, let us define what the Church means by Real

Presence. In the eleventh century, theologian Berengar of Tours taught against the Real Presence. The Church called a series of local councils to clarify her teachings. At the Synod of Rome held in 1059, Berengar's erroneous teachings were rejected and the truth was proclaimed. The synod provided Berengar with an Act of Faith that stated the teaching of the Church: "that the bread and wine that are placed on the altar, after the consecration, are not only a sacrament, but also the true Body and Blood of our Lord Jesus Christ and that they are sensibly, not only in sacrament but in truth, touched and broken by the hands of priests and ground by the teeth of the faithful."[1]

Berengar fell again into error, so in 1079, the Church once more condemned his false teaching and provided another Act of Faith that declared the teaching of the Church:

> that through the mystery of the sacred prayer and the words of our Redeemer the bread and wine that are placed on the altar are substantially changed into the true and proper and living flesh and blood of Jesus Christ, our Lord, and that after consecration it is the true body of Christ that was born of the Virgin and that, offered for the salvation of the world, was suspended on the Cross and that sits at the right hand of the Father, and the true blood of Christ, which was poured out from his side not only through the sign and power of the sacrament, but in its proper nature and in the truth of its substance.[2]

In this dispute, the teaching is clear that the true presence of Christ in the Eucharist means that the Eucharist is substantially the same body and blood of Jesus Christ that was

1 Heinrich Denzinger, *Compendium of Creeds, Definitions, and Declarations on Matters of Faith and Morals,* ed. Peter Hünermann, 43rd ed. (San Francisco, CA: Ignatius Press, 2013), p. 234.

2 Heinrich Denzinger, *Compendium of Creeds*, p. 235.

born of Mary and crucified on the cross. The debates on the Real Presence of Christ in the Eucharist died down until the Protestant revolution.

In response to the rise of Protestantism and its beliefs regarding the Lord's Supper, the Council of Trent published the *Decree on the Sacrament of the Eucharist*. In canon 1 the council taught that "in the sacrament of the Most Holy Eucharist the body and blood . . . is truly, really, and substantially contained."

To understand the definitions of the Synod of Rome and the Council of Trent, we need to understand what is meant by "substantially." In the Aristotelian philosophy used by the majority of Catholic theologians in the medieval and reformation periods, the word "substance" explains what a thing is. Therefore, when we ask what the Eucharist is, the answer is "the body and blood of Christ." It is important to understand that this doesn't mean it is a chunk taken out of Jesus's body. It is the body and blood of Christ, but distinct from the body and blood of Christ that ascended into heaven. The Eucharist is our Lord fully present to us, as substantially present to us as He was present to His apostles during His life on earth.

The Council of Trent also rejected those who say "that he is in it only as in a sign or figure or by his power." So the Catholic Church believes that the Eucharist is the body and blood of Christ not only in sign, figure, and power, but really and truly. The Eucharist is no mere sign or figure. Christ is fully and substantially present. The Eucharist is the living God, the incarnate Second Person of the Blessed Trinity, who was born of the Virgin and crucified on the cross.

In his encyclical *Mysterium Fidei*, Pope St. Paul VI beautifully summarized the Church's teaching on the Real Presence in the Eucharist as spelled out by the various councils:

> This presence is called "real". . . to indicate presence par excellence, because it is substantial and through it Christ becomes present whole and entire, God and man. And so it would be wrong for anyone to try to explain this manner of presence by dreaming up a so-called "pneumatic" nature of the glorious body of Christ that would be present everywhere; or for anyone to limit it to symbolism, as if this most sacred Sacrament were to consist in nothing more than an efficacious sign "of the spiritual presence of Christ and of His intimate union with the faithful, the members of His Mystical Body."[3]

---

3   Pope Paul VI, *Mysterium Fidei*, encyclical, March 9, 1965, no. 39.

5

ST. IGNATIUS OF ANTIOCH

S T. Ignatius of Antioch was the bishop of Antioch in the latter part of the first century. Although we know few details about his life, he was a disciple of St. John the Apostle and was a lifelong friend of fellow bishop St. Polycarp. He was arrested in Antioch and escorted to Rome for martyrdom during Trajan's reign. On the way to Rome, he wrote five letters to the communities he had passed through in his travels, one letter to his friend Polycarp, and one letter to Rome's Christian community. The exact date of his martyrdom is uncertain, but it was likely after the turn of the century.

Letter to the Smyrnaeans

Introduction

Ignatius's *Letter to the Smyrnaeans* was written to the Church at Smyrna, a Greek city on the Aegean coast of Anatolia (modern-day Turkey). Ignatius's friend Polycarp was the bishop of Smyrna, and Ignatius penned a letter to the Church in Smyrna and a separate one to Polycarp while he was in Troas on his way to Rome.

The letter warned the Christians against those who taught the tenants of Docetism. Docetism was an early Christian heresy that fundamentally believed that the material world was evil. Proponents of Docetism asserted that Jesus could not have really taken on flesh and blood and that He did not suffer, die, or rise in the flesh but only appeared to do so. In his polemics against this heresy, we see Ignatius's belief in the Real Presence of Christ in the Eucharist shine through.

Text: Ad Smyrn 6:2–7:1

Now note well those who hold heretical opinions about the grace of Jesus Christ that came to us; note how contrary they are to the mind of God. They have no concern for love, none for the widow, none for the orphan, none for the oppressed, none for the prisoner or the one released, none for the hungry or thirsty. They abstain from Eucharist and prayer, because they refuse to acknowledge that the Eucharist is the flesh of our savior Jesus Christ, which suffered for our sins, and which the Father by His goodness raised up. Therefore those who deny the good gift of God perish in their contentiousness. It would be more to their advantage to love, in order that they might also rise up. It is proper, therefore, to avoid such people and not speak about them either privately or publicly. Do pay attention, however, to the prophets and especially to the gospel, in which the passion has been made clear to us and the resurrection has been accomplished.[1]

Commentary

In classic St. Ignatius style, he makes his point quickly. These people are heretics and are contrary to the mind of God. One clarification is that he is not talking about grace being something other than Jesus Christ. When Ignatius says "heretical opinions about the grace of Jesus Christ," he's not talking directly about heretical opinions about grace but

1   Michael W. Holmes, *The Apostolic Fathers in English* (Grand Rapids, MI: Baker Academic, 2006), pp. 253–55.

rather about Jesus Christ. In this text, "of Jesus Christ" is what is called in Greek the genitive of apposition. The genitive of apposition is when you want to say that two words refer to the same object. For example, John 2:21 uses the genitive of apposition when it clarifies, "But he was speaking of the temple of his body." In this biblical passage, the temple is the body, and the body is the temple. Therefore, in the Letter to the Smyrnaeans, "the grace of Jesus Christ" should not be understood as "Jesus Christ's grace" but rather "the grace, who is Jesus Christ." For Ignatius, this polemic is about Jesus Christ Himself, the core of Christian belief.

After highlighting that these heretics do not live the life of charity that they ought to as Christians, he transitions to the heart of our discussion on the Eucharist. The letter reads, "They abstain from Eucharist and prayer, because they refuse to acknowledge that the Eucharist is the flesh of our savior Jesus Christ, which suffered for our sins, and which the Father by His goodness raised up." After using the life of charity to prove that the Docetists are not to be trusted, the second biggest weapon that Ignatius can find is that they don't celebrate the Eucharist. This point is striking because Ignatius was not trying to prove the Real Presence of Christ in the Eucharist but was using this as a premise to prove that the Docetists were not real Christians. In a contentious situation, premises are what everyone agrees to be unquestionably true. The premises are the unshakable foundation upon which the rest of the argument rests. Therefore, Ignatius's use of the Eucharist being the flesh of Christ as a premise for his argument shows that Ignatius and the Christians in Smyrna universally and unquestionably accepted the teaching.

Ignatius's belief in the Real Presence of Christ in the Eucharist becomes even more evident after analyzing the Greek used in the statement "the Eucharist is the flesh of our savior Jesus Christ, which suffered for our sins, and which the Father by His goodness raised up." The English translation "which" is an accurate one. The Greek word used for "which" (την) is feminine, which means that the "which" refers back not to "Jesus Christ" (in English, the correct pronoun would be "who" in that case) but rather the "flesh." Therefore, Ignatius asserts the Eucharist is the same flesh that suffered on the cross and rose from the dead. His understanding was not that the Eucharist was a mere symbol or that it was only present spiritually or in power but rather that it was the flesh of Christ.

Letter to the Romans

Introduction

Ignatius's *Letter to the Romans* is an elegant and heartfelt plea asking that the Christians in Rome not impede his martyrdom. Ignatius eloquently expresses his desire to imitate the sacrifice of Jesus Christ through his own death. Ignatius considers himself privileged to face martyrdom and begs the Christian community of Rome to think the same. Unlike Ignatius's other letters, he sends the *Letter to the Romans* to a community he has not yet visited. The letter is sent before him to prepare the community for his arrival.

Text: Ad Romanos 7:3

I take no pleasure in corruptible food or the pleasures of this life. I want the bread of God, which is the flesh of Christ who is of the seed of David; and for drink I want his blood, which is incorruptible love.[2]

Commentary

In this passage to the Romans, Ignatius explains what he truly desires. He pleads with the Romans not to stop him from achieving his desire of martyrdom, and even if he in his weakness asks for them to stop his suffering, he says not to allow him to turn back from his course. He wants the will of God and nothing else.

The importance of this passage to our topic is quite straightforward. Ignatius calls the bread of God the flesh of Christ, and he says that he wants to drink Christ's blood. These would be odd things to write if there were not already a common understanding among the Christians in Rome that they eat Christ's flesh and drink His blood.[3] Therefore it is evident the early Christians during Ignatius's time (ca. AD 100) believed that the Eucharist was truly the flesh and blood of Christ.

This passage has clear parallels to the bread of life discourse in John 6, which become even more potent when considering that Ignatius was a disciple of John the Apostle. Therefore, this early Christian text (along with the excerpt from the *Letter to the Smyrnaeans* above) of a disciple of the author of the Gospel of John sheds significant light on the proper interpretation of John 6, as Ignatius had learned

---

2   Holmes, *The Apostolic Fathers,* p. 233.
3   See chapter 3 on the common figurative meaning of eating the flesh and drinking the blood of someone.

his faith from John the Apostle. Ignatius firmly believed in the Eucharist being Christ's flesh and blood, and this passage connects that belief to John 6. Therefore, it is reasonable that John considered the bread of life discourse in his Gospel to be about the Eucharist.

Conclusion/Review

Key Ideas

- Ignatius is a bishop and martyr from the first century who studied under John the Apostle and wrote seven letters as he was escorted to Rome for martyrdom.
- The Smyrnaeans so firmly believed that the Eucharist was the flesh of Christ that Ignatius used it as a premise to refute the Docetist heresy.
- Ignatius used terms and phrases similar to those used in the bread of life discourse in John 6 to speak about the Eucharist, which is evidence that John the Apostle considered the bread of life discourse to be about the Eucharist.

Good Facts and Passages to Memorize

- Ignatius (along with his friend Polycarp) was a student of John the Apostle.
- Ignatius was martyred at the beginning of the second century.
- *Letter to the Smyrnaeans* 6:2: "They [the Docetists] abstain from Eucharist and prayer because they refuse to acknowledge that the Eucharist is the flesh of our savior Jesus Christ,

which suffered for our sins and which the Father by his goodness raised up."

- *Letter to the Romans* 7:3: "I want the bread of God, which is the flesh of Christ who is of the seed of David; and for drink I want his blood, which is incorruptible love."

Effective Questions to Ask When Discussing the Real Presence

- If Ignatius didn't believe in the Real Presence of Christ in the Eucharist, what did he mean in these passages?
- If John, the beloved apostle who sat next to Jesus at the Last Supper, didn't believe that the Eucharist was Jesus's flesh and blood that suffered on the cross and rose from the dead, how did Ignatius adopt that belief, and why was it universally accepted in Smyrna, the city of Polycarp (another of John's disciples)?
- Why did nobody denounce Ignatius's writings if the early Church didn't believe that the Eucharist was really Jesus's flesh and blood?

6

ST. JUSTIN MARTYR

S T. Justin Martyr was born in Flavius Neapolis, a city about thirty miles north of Jerusalem, into a pagan family around the year AD 100. Growing up, he studied the Greek philosophers, but they left him unsatisfied. St. Justin encountered Christianity, and realizing that it answered the questions at the depth of his heart much more capably than the Greek philosophers, he converted to Christianity. He then became the first known Christian philosopher, traveling and teaching Christianity as the "true philosophy." During the reign of Antoninus Pius (AD 138–161), he moved to Rome and started a school. He was denounced to the emperor by his adversaries and was martyred around AD 165 for refusing to sacrifice to the Roman gods.

Only three of his many works are extant: the *Dialogue with Trypho the Jew* and two *Apologies*. Justin wrote the *Dialogue* in the style of a Platonic dialogue between himself and Trypho, a Jew whom Justin encounters shortly after his conversion to Christianity. Throughout the work, Justin shows that the prophecies and all of the Old Testament point to Jesus Christ as the awaited Messiah. An apology in Greek and Roman literature is not a document saying "I'm sorry" but a work that defends a person or group of persons against accusations. For example, an apology was the argument that a lawyer would make on behalf of his client in a court of law. Therefore, Justin's *Apologies* are works that defend the Christians against the many false accusations that were leveled against them by their non-Christian counterparts. These works are of great value to the study of the life and teachings of early Christianity because they are written to an audience that knows almost nothing about Christianity. They defend Christian life and teaching against the attacks that have been leveled against them from the beginning. We will be examining an excerpt from the *First Apology* in which Justin outlines the Mass of the early Christians and their belief in the Eucharist.

Text: First Apology 65–66

Ch. 65

But we, after we have thus washed him who has been convinced and has assented to our teaching, bring him to the place where those who are called brethren are assembled, in order that we may offer hearty prayers in common for ourselves and for the baptized [illuminated] person, and for all others in every place, that we may be counted worthy, now that we have learned the truth, by our works also to be found good citizens and keepers of the commandments, so that we may be saved with an everlasting salvation. Having ended the prayers, we salute one another with a kiss. There is then brought to the president of the brethren bread and a cup of wine mixed with water; and he taking them, gives praise and glory to the Father of the universe, through the name of the Son and of the Holy Ghost, and offers thanks at considerable length for our being counted worthy to receive these things at His hands. And when he has concluded the prayers and thanksgivings, all the people present express their assent by saying Amen. This word Amen answers in the Hebrew language to γένοιτο [so be it]. And when the president has given thanks, and all the

people have expressed their assent, those who are called by
us deacons give to each of those present to partake of the
bread and wine mixed with water over which the thanksgiving
was pronounced, and to those who are absent they carry away
a portion.

Ch. 66

And this food is called among us Εὐχαριστία [the Eucharist],
of which no one is allowed to partake but the man who
believes that the things which we teach are true, and who
has been washed with the washing that is for the remission
of sins, and unto regeneration, and who is so living as Christ
has enjoined. For not as common bread and common drink
do we receive these; but in like manner as Jesus Christ our
Saviour, having been made flesh by the Word of God, had
both flesh and blood for our salvation, so likewise have we
been taught that the food which is blessed by the prayer of His
word, and from which our blood and flesh by transmutation are
nourished, is the flesh and blood of that Jesus who was made
flesh. For the apostles, in the memoirs composed by them,
which are called Gospels, have thus delivered unto us what
was enjoined upon them; that Jesus took bread, and when He
had given thanks, said, This do in remembrance of Me, this is
My body; and that, after the same manner, having taken the
cup and given thanks, He said, This is My blood; and gave it
to them alone.[1]

Commentary

These two chapters of Justin's *First Apology* come right after
an explanation and defense of Christian baptism. The first
sentence of chapter 65 moves the scene from baptism into
the celebration of the Lord's Supper. This passage depicts
the early form of the Mass, and it is striking how much it

---

1   James Donaldson and Alexander Roberts, *Ante-Nicene Christian
     Library: Translations of the Writings of the Fathers Down to A. D.
     325* (Edinburgh: T. and T. Clark), pp. 63–65.

corresponds to today's liturgy from the Prayers of the Faithful through the rest of the Mass. It is valuable to examine the parallel because it gives credence to the continuity of Catholic teaching and practice throughout the centuries:

Justin's *First Apology's* Correspondence to the Current Form of Mass		
First Apology Quote	Part of Mass Today	Explanation
"Having ended the prayers, we salute one another with a kiss."	The Sign (or "Kiss") of Peace	The Sign of Peace today comes right before Communion and is typically done as a handshake, but a ritual form of an embrace called "The Kiss of Peace" is still preserved among the clergy.
"There is then brought to the president of the brethren bread and a cup of wine mixed with water."	Presentation and Preparation of the Gifts	The people bring forward bread and wine in procession, and the deacon mixes the water and wine into the chalice and presents it to the priest.

Justin's *First Apology's* Correspondence to the Current Form of Mass		
First Apology Quote	**Part of Mass Today**	**Explanation**
"and he taking them, gives praise and glory to the Father of the universe, through the name of the Son and of the Holy Ghost, and offers thanks at considerable length for our being counted worthy to receive these things at His hands."	The Eucharistic Prayer	The priest alone prays at length and consecrates the Eucharist (gk. "Thanksgiving").
"All the people present express their assent by saying Amen."	The people's response "Amen" at the end of the Eucharistic Prayer.	
"those who are called by us deacons give to each of those present to partake of the bread and wine mixed with water over which the thanksgiving was pronounced"	The Communion Rite	The people receive Communion from the priest and deacon, and if more ministers are required, laypeople can assist in distributing Communion.

Justin's *First Apology's* Correspondence to the Current Form of Mass		
First Apology Quote	Part of Mass Today	Explanation
"and to those who are absent they carry away a portion."	Communion to the Sick	Still today, the Catholic Church practices bringing Communion to those who are unable to attend Mass.

Chapter 66 focuses more directly on this book's topic: the Real Presence of Christ in the Eucharist. The first line uses the word "Eucharist" to describe the Christians' gathering and the moment in which they commemorate the Lord's Supper, which supports the interpretations of the biblical passages regarding "giving thanks" in the first section of this book. It is also notable that the early Christians had the same restrictions on who can receive the Eucharist as the Catholic Church does today: "of which no one is allowed to partake but the man who believes that the things which we teach are true, and who has been washed with the washing that is for the remission of sins, and unto regeneration, and who is so living as Christ has enjoined"; namely, they must believe what the Church believes, be baptized, and live the Christian life (i.e., be in the state of grace). Up to this point, we can see a clear correlation between how the early Church and the Catholic Church today *act* concerning the Eucharist. Now we turn to what the early Church *believed* about the Eucharist.

Justin set up a parallel in his explanation of the Eucharist: "in like manner as Jesus Christ . . . had both flesh and blood, . . . so likewise . . . the food . . . is the flesh and blood of that Jesus who was made flesh." Justin explains that the Eucharist is Jesus's flesh and blood in the same manner that Jesus had flesh and blood. Therefore, if we believe that Jesus had real flesh and blood, then according to Justin, the Eucharist is Jesus's real flesh and blood. This statement of Justin is even more poignant when we consider the historical context and purpose of this *Apology*. Christians had been falsely accused of being cannibals, which was one reason why there was a cultural bias against them. Justin's purpose in writing this work was to remove any misunderstandings regarding Christianity and put the Christian community into a good light before the eyes of the secular rulers of that time. If the early Christians didn't believe that the Eucharist was truly the body and blood of Christ, it would have been an opportune time for Justin to set the record straight and let everyone know that the Eucharist was not real flesh and blood but simply a symbolic presence, a spiritual presence, or anything but Jesus's flesh and blood. But Justin didn't do that. He explained that the Christians believe that the Eucharist is flesh and blood as much as they believe that Jesus had flesh and blood.

Justin then explained why Christians believe that the Eucharist is truly the body and blood of Christ. He argued that this belief was taught to the Christians by the apostles: "For the apostles, in the memoirs composed by them, which are called Gospels, have thus delivered unto us what was enjoined upon them." He then cited the institution narratives (explained in the first section of this book) as the biblical foundation for his argument. The *First Apology* rounds out Justin's teaching on the Eucharist as being thoroughly Catholic. The Catholic Church celebrates the Eucharist with the same pattern that the early Christians did and has preserved the same faith regarding the Eucharist to this day.

Conclusion/Review

Key Ideas

- Justin Martyr is a Christian philosopher from the first half of the second century, born in modern-day Palestine and educated in Rome.
- Justin's account of the Eucharistic celebration in the early Church corresponds closely to today's celebration of the Mass.
- Justin believes that the Eucharist is the flesh and blood of Christ, just as Jesus had flesh and blood.

Good Facts and Passages to Memorize

- The early Church had the same restrictions on the Eucharist's reception that the Catholic Church has today.
- *First Apology*, ch. 66: "in like manner as Jesus Christ our Saviour, having been made flesh by the Word of God, had both flesh and blood for our salvation, so likewise have we been taught that the food which is blessed by the prayer of His word, and from which our blood and flesh by transmutation are nourished, is the flesh and blood of that Jesus who was made flesh."

- Justin stated that the Christians' belief in the Eucharist comes from the Apostles.

Effective Questions to Ask When Discussing the Real Presence

- In the *First Apology,* Justin clarifies misunderstandings and defends Christians against false rumors. One of those rumors was that Christians were cannibals. If he did not believe the Eucharist was actually the flesh and blood of Christ, why didn't Justin explain that in this work?
- Could the apostles' teachings have been so misunderstood in both Rome and Judea by the time that Justin was alive (first half of the second century)?

7

ST. IRENAEUS OF LYONS

S T. Irenaeus is the next Father of the Church who makes clear and strong statements about the Real Presence of Christ in the Eucharist. Born around the year AD 130 in Smyrna (the town of St. Polycarp; modern-day Izmir in Turkey), he listened to the preaching of Polycarp, who was a disciple of St. John, the apostle and evangelist. He grew up in a Christian family and was ordained a priest. While serving in the modern-day French city of Lyons, a persecution broke out. His fellow priests sent Irenaeus to Rome with a letter for the pope. When he returned to Lyons, he was made bishop of the city, succeeding the bishop martyr St. Pothinus. St. Irenaeus's thought is particularly important because of his lived experience in three of the major regions of Christianity at the time: Smyrna, Rome, and Gaul. His writings attest to the shared belief of three distant areas of Christianity that reflect vastly different social, historical, and political contexts. In more simple terms, because St. Irenaeus lived in several places, if he believed the Real Presence, then Christians everywhere probably believed in it too.

St. Irenaeus's most famous work is *On the Detection and Overthrow of the So-Called Gnosis*, more commonly referred to as *Against Heresies*. He wrote it around the year

180 when he was already a bishop in Lyons. It is a work dedicated to cataloging the Gnostic sects and other heresies (book I), rebutting their errors (books II–III), and teaching the true Christian faith (books IV–V). Irenaeus uses three sources to refute the heresies and prove the true faith: the Scriptures, the tradition (or handing down) of the teaching of the apostles, and what is taught by the successors of the apostles (i.e., the bishops). Our study will look at three sections of books IV and V in which Irenaeus speaks of the Eucharist and what the Christians believe about it.

Against Heresies

Book IV, ch. 18.4–5

Those, again, who maintain that the things around us originated from apostasy, ignorance, and passion, do, while offering unto Him the fruits of ignorance, passion, and apostasy, sin against their Father, rather subjecting Him to insult than giving Him thanks. But how can they be consistent with themselves, [when they say] that the bread over which thanks have been given is the body of their Lord, and the cup His blood, if they do not call Himself the Son of the Creator of the world, that is, His Word, through whom the wood fructifies, and the fountains gush forth, and the earth gives first the blade, then the ear, then the full grain in the ear.

Then, again, how can they say that the flesh, which is nourished with the body of the Lord and with His blood, goes to corruption, and does not partake of life? Let them, therefore, either alter their opinion, or cease from offering the things just mentioned. But our opinion is in accordance with the Eucharist, and the Eucharist in turn establishes our opinion. For we offer to Him His own, announcing consistently the fellowship and union of the flesh and Spirit. For as the bread, which is produced from the earth, when it receives the invocation of God, is no longer common bread, but the Eucharist, consisting of two realities, earthly and heavenly; so also our bodies, when they receive the Eucharist, are no longer corruptible, having the hope of the resurrection to eternity.[1]

Commentary

Book IV, chapter 18 is dedicated to refuting those who claimed that the God who created the world was different or even at odds with the God who saved the world. To refute this particular error, St. Irenaeus references a common Christian practice at the time: the celebration of the Eucharist. The excerpted text above is from the middle of his argument.

The first thing to clarify is what Irenaeus is talking about when he says, "Those, again, who maintain that the things around us originated from apostasy, ignorance, and passion." Many sects[2] of Gnosticism (the early Christian heresy that *Against Heresies* is principally dedicated to refuting) used mythological storytelling to explain God's reality and the world's creation. According to some of these myths, the material world resulted from the apostasy, ignorance, and passion of the demiurge (who, according to Gnosticism, is one of the members of the hierarchical structure of divine beings from whom the material world originated).

Irenaeus points out the self-contradiction of offering God something from the material world if the material world is

---

1 Alexander Roberts, James Donaldson, and A. Cleveland Coxe, eds., *Ante-Nicene Fathers*, Vol. 1, trans. Alexander Roberts and William Rambaut (Buffalo, NY: Christian Literature Publishing Co., 1885).

2 Gnosticism was not a unified set of beliefs, but rather a group of heresies with fundamental similarities that were propagated by a number of independent preachers.

the effect of a rebellion against God: "[They] sin against their Father, rather subjecting Him to insult than giving Him thanks." Taking part in anything material would be cooperating with the rebellious demiurge, so how can you say that you are giving thanks to God by offering Him something material? Moreover, Irenaeus clarifies that they are self-contradictory for calling the bread and wine over which the prayer of blessing is said the flesh and blood of the Son—still two material things—if they do not call the Son the Creator of the world.

At the beginning of paragraph 5, Irenaeus makes another stab at the Gnostic belief: "Then, again, how can they say that the flesh, which is nourished with the body of the Lord and with His blood, goes to corruption, and does not partake of life?" This argument concerns the belief in the resurrection of the body of the believer. Irenaeus says human flesh "is nourished with the body of the Lord and with His blood." The logic here is that a material thing, human flesh, is nourished by a material thing, the body and blood of the Lord, and that nourishment brings about the effect of giving life. This logic aligns well with the Catholic Church's teaching that Jesus Christ's body and blood are present even materially in the Eucharist. It also echoes what we discussed in the bread of life discourse in John 6 concerning the Eucharist's effects on those who receive it.

Next, Irenaeus clearly states that the universal Church's belief in the Eucharist is his lifeboat amid the sea of heresies that he is refuting: "But our opinion is in accordance with the Eucharist, and the Eucharist in turn establishes our opinion." He then repeats the two arguments explained in the above paragraphs: "For as the bread, which is produced from the earth, when it receives the invocation of God, is no longer common bread, but the Eucharist, consisting of two realities, earthly and heavenly; so also our bodies, when they receive the Eucharist, are no longer corruptible, having the hope of the resurrection to eternity."

Book IV, ch. 33.2

2. Moreover, he shall also examine the doctrine of Marcion, [inquiring] how he holds that there are two gods, separated from each other by an infinite distance. Or how can he be good who draws away men that do not belong to him from him who made them, and calls them into his own kingdom? And why is his goodness, which does not save all [thus], defective? Also, why does he, indeed, seem to be good as respects men, but most unjust with regard to him who made men, inasmuch as he deprives him of his possessions? Moreover, how could the Lord, with any justice, if He belonged to another father, have acknowledged the bread to be His body, while He took it from that creation to which we belong, and affirmed the mixed cup to be His blood? And why did He acknowledge Himself to be the Son of man, if He had not gone through that birth which belongs to a human being? How, too, could He forgive us those sins for which we are answerable to our Maker and God? And how, again, supposing that He was not flesh, but was a man merely in appearance, could He have been crucified, and could blood and water have issued from His pierced side? What body, moreover, was it that those who buried Him consigned to the tomb? And what was that which rose again from the dead?

Commentary

Book 4, chapter 33 of *Against Heresies* focuses on proving that the God of the Old Testament is the same God of the New Testament. Paragraph 2 starts an attack against Marcion, who believed that there was one evil creator god and one good savior god who were separated from each other and at war with each other. Irenaeus asks a series of questions that elucidate the absurdity of such a claim, and nestled in the middle of them is a question about the Eucharist: "Moreover, how could the Lord, with any justice, if He belonged to another father, have acknowledged the bread to be His body, while He took it from that creation to which we belong, and affirmed the mixed cup to be His blood?"

The argument is fundamentally the same as that of the first text we looked at: if Jesus wasn't the creator God, why did He use material things in the Eucharist?[3] First, according to Gnostic claims, those were the things of the opposing evil god, and second, that's stealing and stealing is unjust. Once again, the use of the Church's faith in the Eucharist as the undoubtable proof that the Savior also created the material world loudly proclaims the universal and certain faith in the real and material presence of Christ in the Eucharist among the early Christians.

It is also worth noting the other irrefutable doctrines that the Eucharist is nestled among: God's victory over evil, the reality of hell, God's goodness, the Incarnation, the forgiveness of sins, the crucifixion, burial, and resurrection of the Lord. In the life of the early Church, the Eucharist was considered so fundamental and so undeniably the body and blood of our Lord that Irenaeus listed it alongside such doctrines.

---

3   The "mixed cup" that is referenced is the same cup that is used in the Mass. From the earliest times, the priest or deacon has mixed a little bit of water into the wine before the consecration.

Book V, ch. 2.2–3

2. But vain in every respect are they who despise the entire dispensation of God, and disallow the salvation of the flesh, and treat with contempt its regeneration, maintaining that it is not capable of incorruption. But if this indeed does not attain salvation, then neither did the Lord redeem us with His blood, nor is the cup of the Eucharist the communion of His blood, nor the bread which we break the communion of His body. For blood can only come from veins and flesh, and whatsoever else makes up the substance of man, such as the Word of God was actually made. By His own blood He redeemed us, as also His apostle declares, in whom we have redemption through His blood, even the remission of sins. And as we are His members, we are also nourished by means of the creation (and He Himself grants the creation to us, for He causes His sun to rise, and sends rain when He wills). He has acknowledged the cup (which is a part of the creation) as His own blood, from which He bedews our blood; and the bread (also a part of the creation) He has established as His own body, from which He gives increase to our bodies.

3. When, therefore, the mingled cup and the manufactured bread receives the Word of God, and the Eucharist of the blood and the body of Christ is made, from which things the substance of our flesh is increased and supported, how can they affirm that the flesh is incapable of receiving the gift of God, which is life eternal, which [flesh] is nourished from the body and blood of the Lord, and is a member of Him?—even as the blessed Paul declares in his Epistle to the Ephesians, that we are members of His body, of His flesh, and of His bones. He does not speak these words of some spiritual and invisible man, for a spirit has not bones nor flesh; but [he refers to] that dispensation [by which the Lord became] an actual man, consisting of flesh, and nerves, and bones—that [flesh] which is nourished by the cup which is His blood, and receives increase from the bread which is His body. And just as a cutting from the vine planted in the ground fructifies in its season, or as a grain of wheat falling into the earth and

becoming decomposed, rises with manifold increase by the
Spirit of God, who contains all things, and then, through the
wisdom of God, serves for the use of men, and having received
the Word of God, becomes the Eucharist, which is the body
and blood of Christ; so also our bodies, being nourished by it,
and deposited in the earth, and suffering decomposition there,
shall rise at their appointed time.

Commentary

In chapter 2 of book V, Irenaeus defends and teaches the
Christian doctrine of the body's physical resurrection. In
paragraph 2, Irenaeus starts his argument from the Eucharist, which is the following: Jesus Christ redeemed our
physical bodies by His physical body and blood. We know
that He had a physical body and blood because the Eucharist is His physical body and blood.

Once again, we have the shocking argument structure in
which Irenaeus uses the universal belief in the Real Presence
of Christ in the Eucharist as the proof for something that is
now considered undebatable: the bodily resurrection. At the
time of Irenaeus, the Eucharist was undebatable, but people
doubted whether bodily resurrection was possible. Unfortunately, many Christians have now reversed the equation and
doubt the Real Presence of Christ in the Eucharist.

The parallel structure of paragraph 3 is the most unam-
biguous statement in Irenaeus's works showing that he
believed Jesus's body and blood to be present in the Eucharist in the exact way that it was present in His fleshly body.
Making a comparison to the Eucharist, Irenaeus says, "even
as the blessed Paul declares in his Epistle to the Ephesians,
that we are members of His body, of His flesh, and of His
bones. He does not speak these words of some spiritual and

invisible man, for a spirit has not bones nor flesh; but [he refers to] that dispensation [by which the Lord became] an actual man, consisting of flesh, and nerves, and bones." When that phrase is coupled in the same paragraph with sayings like "that [flesh] which is nourished by the cup which is His blood, and receives increase from the bread which is His body" and "[the bread and wine] having received the Word of God, becomes the Eucharist, which is the body and blood of Christ," it is difficult to think that he believed anything other than what the Catholic Church teaches about Jesus Christ's presence in the Eucharist.

Conclusion

Key Ideas

- Irenaeus lived in three major regions of Christianity (Smyrna, Rome, and Lyons) throughout his lifetime, so he is a testament to what the universal Church taught and believed in the second century.
- Irenaeus considered the Real Presence of Christ to be so beyond doubt that he used it to argue against other heresies.
- Irenaeus believed the Eucharist to be physically the body and blood of Jesus in the same way that his fleshly body was physically his body.

Good Facts and Passages to Memorize

- "But our opinion is in accordance with the Eucharist, and the Eucharist in turn establishes our opinion" (*Against Heresies*, IV, 18, 5).

- "He has acknowledged the cup (which is a part of the creation) as His own blood, from which He bedews our blood; and the bread (also a part of the creation) He has established as His own body, from which He gives increase to our bodies" (*Against Heresies*, V, 2, 2).
- The bread and wine "having received the Word of God, becomes the Eucharist, which is the body and blood of Christ" (*Against Heresies,* V, 2, 3).

Effective Questions to Ask When Discussing the Real Presence

- If some of the Christian communities that Irenaeus visited didn't believe in the Eucharist, why did Irenaeus consider it something so undoubtable that he used it to argue against other heresies?
- If Irenaeus didn't believe that the Eucharist was really the body and blood of Jesus, how do you make his arguments in these texts make sense?
- Irenaeus was a disciple of Polycarp who was a disciple of John the Apostle. Is it reasonable that Jesus's teachings on the Eucharist, from the bread of life discourse and the Last Supper, were already so corrupted by the time they got to St. Irenaeus that he did not understand what the Eucharist actually was?

8

ST. CYRIL OF JERUSALEM

L ITTLE is known about the early life of St. Cyril of Jerusalem. He was born around AD 314 in or near the city of Jerusalem. In AD 350, he succeeded St. Maximus as bishop of Jerusalem. He died around AD 387. The first thing to notice is that a significant period passed between the life of St. Irenaeus and St. Cyril. This gap is due to several reasons: Firstly, there are not many extant works from the theologian saints of the early to mid-third century due to Roman persecution of Christians in that century. Secondly, the heresy of Arianism, which claimed that Jesus was not fully God, entered the theological arena in the late third century, and the majority of writings of the time focused on that debate. Thirdly, we intentionally skipped over St. Hilary of Poitiers because his work adds little to the discussion. Meanwhile, the era of St. Cyril's writings allowed the Church to recover from the shift caused by the Edict of Milan in AD 313, which proves the continued belief in the Real Presence of Christ in the Eucharist even after such a significant change.

His most famous work is his *Catechetical Lectures*, which St. Cyril gave in AD 347, shortly before being made bishop of Jerusalem. They are made up of twenty-three lectures, eighteen delivered to the region's catechumens during Lent and before they received the sacraments of Baptism,

Confirmation, and Communion, and five delivered to the
new Christians after having received the sacraments. These
are important documents due to their sacramental theology,
their depiction of Jerusalem's liturgy, and the historical
and topographical notes concerning Jerusalem and the surrounding area at the time of Cyril.

Cyril's twenty-second catechetical lecture comments on
Paul's First Letter to the Corinthians 11:23, which is Paul's
account of the words of institution at the Last Supper. This
lecture focuses on the Eucharist and what the new Christians have received in it.

Catechetical Lecture 22

1 Cor 11:23: I received of the Lord that which also I delivered
unto you, how that the Lord Jesus, in the night in which He
was betrayed, took bread, etc.

1. Even of itself the teaching of the Blessed Paul is
sufficient to give you a full assurance concerning those Divine
Mysteries, of which having been deemed worthy, you have
become of the same body and blood with Christ. For you have
just heard him say distinctly, That our Lord Jesus Christ in the
night in which He was betrayed, took bread, and when He had
given thanks He broke it, and gave to His disciples, saying,
Take, eat, this is My Body: and having taken the cup and
given thanks, He said, Take, drink, this is My Blood. Since
then He Himself declared and said of the Bread, This is My
Body, who shall dare to doubt any longer? And since He has
Himself affirmed and said, This is My Blood, who shall ever
hesitate, saying, that it is not His blood?

2. He once in Cana of Galilee, turned the water into
wine, akin to blood, and is it incredible that He should have
turned wine into blood? When called to a bodily marriage,
He miraculously wrought that wonderful work; and on the
children of the bride-chamber, shall He not much rather be

acknowledged to have bestowed the fruition of His Body and Blood?

3. Wherefore with full assurance let us partake as of the Body and Blood of Christ: for in the figure of Bread is given to you His Body, and in the figure of Wine His Blood; that you by partaking of the Body and Blood of Christ, may be made of the same body and the same blood with Him. For thus we come to bear Christ in us, because His Body and Blood are distributed through our members; thus it is that, according to the blessed Peter, we become partakers of the divine nature.

4. Christ on a certain occasion discoursing with the Jews said, Unless you eat My flesh and drink My blood, you have no life in you. They not having heard His saying in a spiritual sense were offended, and went back, supposing that He was inviting them to eat flesh.

5. In the Old Testament also there was show-bread; but this, as it belonged to the Old Testament, has come to an end; but in the New Testament there is Bread of heaven, and a Cup of salvation, sanctifying soul and body; for as the Bread corresponds to our body, so is the Word appropriate to our soul.

6. Consider therefore the Bread and the Wine not as bare elements, for they are, according to the Lord's declaration, the Body and Blood of Christ; for even though sense suggests this to you, yet let faith establish you. Judge not the matter from the taste, but from faith be fully assured without misgiving, that the Body and Blood of Christ have been vouchsafed to you.

7. Also the blessed David shall advise you the meaning of this, saying, You have prepared a table before me in the presence of them that afflict me. What he says, is to this effect: Before Your coming, the evil spirits prepared a table for men, polluted and defiled and full of devilish influence; but since Your coming. O Lord, You have prepared a table before me. When the man says to God, You have prepared before me a table, what other does he indicate but that mystical and spiritual Table, which God has prepared for us over against, that is, contrary and in opposition to the evil spirits? And very

truly; for that had communion with devils, but this, with God. You have anointed my head with oil. With oil He anointed your head upon your forehead, for the seal which you have of God; that you may be made the engraving of the signet, Holiness unto God. And your cup intoxicates me, as very strong. You see that cup here spoken of, which Jesus took in His hands, and gave thanks, and said, This is My blood, which is shed for many for the remission of sins.

8. Therefore Solomon also, hinting at this grace, says in Ecclesiastes, Come hither, eat your bread with joy (that is, the spiritual bread; Come hither, he calls with the call to salvation and blessing), and drink your wine with a merry heart (that is, the spiritual wine); and let oil be poured out upon your head you see he alludes even to the mystic Chrism); and let your garments be always white, for the Lord is well pleased with your works; for before you came to Baptism, your works were vanity of vanities. But now, having put off your old garments, and put on those which are spiritually white, you must be continually robed in white: of course we mean not this, that you are always to wear white raiment; but you must be clad in the garments that are truly white and shining and spiritual, that you may say with the blessed Esaias, My soul shall be joyful in my God; for He has clothed me with a garment of salvation, and put a robe of gladness around me.

9. Having learned these things, and been fully assured that the seeming bread is not bread, though sensible to taste, but the Body of Christ; and that the seeming wine is not wine, though the taste will have it so, but the Blood of Christ; and that of this David sung of old, saying, And bread strengthens man's heart, to make his face to shine with oil, strengthen your heart, by partaking thereof as spiritual, and make the face of your soul to shine. And so having it unveiled with a pure conscience, may you reflect as a mirror the glory of the Lord, and proceed from glory to glory, in Christ Jesus our Lord:— To whom be honour, and might, and glory, for ever and ever. Amen.[1]

1   Philip Schaff and Henry Wace, eds., *Nicene and Post-Nicene Fathers, Second Series*, Vol. 7, trans. Edwin Hamilton Gifford (Buffalo, NY:

Commentary

The first paragraph of Cyril's twenty-second catechetical lecture starts with an exhortation to faith in the words of institution. Cyril recalls the words of St. Paul to the listeners and asks, "Since then He Himself declared and said of the Bread, This is My Body, who shall dare to doubt any longer? And since He has Himself affirmed and said, This is My Blood, who shall ever hesitate, saying, that it is not His blood?" The structure of this paragraph reveals that Cyril understands how difficult it is to believe in the Eucharist. He starts by urging his listeners to trust the words of God. If God has said it, who could doubt?

Next, Cyril uses the miracle at the wedding at Cana as evidence that Jesus does have the power to transform something from one thing into another. At Cana, Jesus turned water into wine. Cyril asks if Jesus can turn water into wine, "is it incredible that He should have turned wine into blood?" Cyril also points out other similarities between the wedding at Cana and the Eucharist: First, wine kind of looks like blood. And more theologically, "when called to a bodily marriage, He miraculously wrought that wonderful work; and on the children of the bride-chamber, shall He not much rather be acknowledged to have bestowed the fruition of His Body and Blood?" This passage, more simply put, means that Jesus gave wine to those who were at the wedding in Cana, so it is fitting that He should give His body and blood to Christians, who are children of the Church, His Bride.

Christian Literature Publishing Co., 1894).

In paragraphs 3 and 4, Cyril addresses what are now
called the Eucharistic species or the accidents of bread and
wine. He exhorts the new Christians to receive Christ's
body and blood, which are "in the figure of Bread" and
"in the figure of Wine." This emphasis is made clear when
read in light of paragraph 4 as Cyril mentions those who
left Jesus after the bread of life discourse because they did
not understand "His saying in a spiritual sense." Here, one
could read Cyril's words "spiritual sense" as meaning "not
real" or "merely figurative," but that reading is contradic-
tory to the conclusion of the text when Cyril clearly says
"that the seeming bread is not bread, though sensible to
taste, but the Body of Christ; and that the seeming wine
is not wine, though the taste will have it so, but the Blood
of Christ." So the proper understanding of Cyril's use of
"spiritual sense" is that the Eucharist does not have the
appearances of flesh but rather the appearances and external characteristics of bread, which is precisely what the
Catholic Church teaches.

The following paragraphs include a series of Old Testament references showing how God prefigured and
foreshadowed the Eucharist through various things: the
showbread, the "table before me" of psalm 23, and Ecclesiastes. Throughout these paragraphs, Cyril emphasizes that
the Eucharistic species of bread and wine are the body and
blood of Christ and that when we receive what seems to
be bread and wine, we are indeed receiving the body and
blood of Christ.

The last paragraph sums up the teaching of the rest of
the lecture, saying, "Having learned these things, and been
fully assured that the seeming bread is not bread, though

sensible to taste, but the Body of Christ; and that the seeming wine is not wine, though the taste will have it so, but the Blood of Christ." Cyril then exhorts his listeners to receive the Eucharist and allow the glory of the Lord to shine through them.

Conclusion

Key Ideas

- Cyril's *Catechetical Lectures* shows that through the persecutions of the Church in the third century and the legalization of Christianity in the first part of the fourth century, the teaching of the Church on the Eucharist remained the same.
- Cyril distinguishes between the reality of the body and blood in the Eucharist and the appearances of bread and wine sensed by the recipient.
- When Cyril uses the term "spiritual sense," he does not mean "not real." Rather, he uses his wording to explain the phenomenon that what the senses perceive to be bread and wine is, in fact, the body and blood of Christ.

Good Facts and Passages to Memorize

- "Since then He Himself declared and said of the Bread, This is My Body, who shall dare to doubt any longer? And since He has Himself affirmed and said, This is My Blood, who shall ever hesitate, saying, that it is not His blood?" (*Catechetical Lectures* 22, 1).

- "Wherefore with full assurance let us partake as of the Body and Blood of Christ: for in the figure of Bread is given to you His Body, and in the figure of Wine His Blood" (*Catechetical Lectures* 22, 3).
- "Having learned these things, and been fully assured that the seeming bread is not bread, though sensible to taste, but the Body of Christ; and that the seeming wine is not wine, though the taste will have it so, but the Blood of Christ" (*Catechetical Lectures* 22, 9).

Effective Questions to Ask When Discussing the Real Presence

- Cyril of Jerusalem's teaching on the Eucharist coincides nicely with Irenaeus's teaching and the Catholic Church's current teaching on the Eucharist. If the Catholic Church went wrong, when and how did it go wrong?
- If you read catechetical lecture 22 as a whole, is there any way to understand the Eucharist as not being the body and blood of Christ?

PART III

WHAT DOES SCIENCE SAY?

9

MIRACLES AND
TRANSUBSTANTIATION

SCIENCE and miracles appear to be at odds with each other, seemingly incapable of belonging in the same sentence together. Science, or at least *modern* science as we know it today, is about quantifying the motion of physical objects in the natural world. Physics measures rates as objects move through the universe. Chemistry measures changes as atoms bond with each other. Biology measures patterns among living things. Miracles? They measure nothing. They override all of science. Miracles are individual and unique events that, of their nature, do not follow the laws of physics, chemistry, or biology. So how, then, is anyone supposed to talk about Eucharistic miracles in light of science?

The answer is to step back from our knowledge of the physical realm of nature and take in a greater landscape of reality, one that includes the supernatural. Nature seen in its proper context is the creation of God, His handiwork, held in existence in every moment by God. A more advanced faith perspective makes it possible to see that God, who holds creation in His hand, can also be compelled by love to act beyond His usual order and show us He is truly present among us. Miracles are simply the logical conclusion of faith in a rational Creator.

Miracles

Determinism is the idea that the order in nature is absolute whereby everything has a fundamental microphysical explanation for all time. Since the very beginning, determinism assumes that the first particles have been causing the movement and change in successive particles. The logic of determinism taken to its fullest conclusion means that humans do not have free will because every thought is merely the action of neurons in the brain acting according to the laws of physics and that those thoughts were predestined since time began.

The assumption that this is all there is to the world is axiomatic. Because their world view does not accommodate the supernatural or spiritual realm, atheists are compelled by their own logic to adopt this view. The unsatisfying conclusion of this view, however, ultimately contradicts the very defining characteristic of being an atheist. If there is no free will, there is no free thought. The atheist is left to find answers limited to science.

The believer's intellect is not so chained. He understands that science, the study of nature, is ultimately and pervasively the study of God's handiwork. If science studies God's creation, then the believer accepts that God exists before he ever explores science. This fuller logic is how St. Thomas Aquinas starts off his famous *Summa Theologiae* (question 2) by explaining how science is the best demonstration for the existence of God, quoting St. Paul the Apostle: "The invisible things of him are clearly seen, being understood by the things that are made" (Rom 1:20). We pray the same in the Creed:

> I believe in one God,
> the Father almighty,
> maker of heaven and earth,
> of all things visible and invisible.

You might wonder if God contradicts Himself by violating His own laws of physics. Think of it like this: Imagine there is a father who loves his family immensely. He provides for them and guides them, and as the head of household, he establishes rules for the family. There is order in his part of the universe. (Since we are talking about a man instead God, it makes sense to say "his part" of the universe.) To the children's chagrin, one of these rules involves ice cream before dinner. Dad has declared that it is too messy and appetites will be ruined if ice cream is eaten before dinner. He deems it good for the kids to appreciate what Mom cooks. This steadfast rule is considered as firm as the law of universal gravitation.

However, let's say that one evening Mom calls Dad at work before he heads home. Mom notices the daughter feeling rejected and unloved because of something that happened to her at school. She was picked on by her friends and feeling very down. To make matters worse, her siblings left her out of the game they were playing that evening at home. The daughter was hurting, and although Dad trusts her to rise above the difficulty, he nevertheless wishes to let her know he is there for her. So Dad decides to override the ice cream rule for that night because he wants to show his love to his daughter in a special way, a personal love that goes beyond merely providing for the family and being the lawmaker of the home. What does Dad do? He comes home from work with many ice cream flavors and even fills her bowl so full it will take at least half an hour to sit down and finish it—just this once. Dad delights in seeing his daughter's happiness. The smile on her face, the awe, the hope is worth a world of ice cream. Sure, there are rules, but there is more to life than rules. Only a father who loves his children enough to implement good rules would also choose to work the extraordinary gift *occasionally* to send a message of unmistakable love to his children. How could he not?

This is what it is like when God works miracles for the sake of our salvation. The usual course of things is uniquely interrupted, and it captures our attention in an awe-inspiring way. God communicates with us in many ways, but when He works a miracle, He is making Himself known in a very personal way tailored to the individuals and the situations. And just as the father surprises his daughter with an ice cream treat, when God works a miracle, He does not violate nor change the rules of nature. Miracles are supernatural, beyond nature. Miracles assert the unity of the natural and the supernatural. The gift of a miracle is a small revelation, a glimpse of the greater truth of the total reality. Children need order in the home, but there is so much more to raising a family or building a kingdom. Science depends on order in the universe, but that order is not all there is either. This greater truth is believed with a greater love. God works miracles because He loves us.

St. Thomas Aquinas in the thirteenth century quoted St. Augustine from the fourth century on the definition

of miracles. St. Augustine said, "Where God does anything against that order of nature which we know and are
accustomed to observe, we call it a miracle."[1] Because we
observe order in nature, it seems like a miracle is contrary
to nature, something beyond nature. If you are an atheist, a
miracle seems like something that is *impossible* in nature
and therefore not possible at all. But truly, since God cannot act against Himself, God is not breaking nature's rules
that He created. When God works a miracle, He is acting
within the realm of what is natural to Him in what we might
call the "supreme law of nature," meaning that God created
everything and holds all things in existence. When Augustine uses the words "which we know" in his description of
a miracle, he says that miracles are actions by God against
the order "which we know" but not against the order which
God knows. Those words beg some questions though, and
it is useful to examine this idea before tackling Eucharistic
miracles and their scientific studies.

Imagine if you are in a restaurant with a friend, and your
friend levitates out of her seat and flies around the room.
That event would be against the order "which we know" in
nature. It is not natural, predictable, nor expected that a person would begin to float in the air. We would surely call this
a miracle! It would mean that God chose to make someone
float in the air for the sake of our salvation, and God is perfectly capable of causing that to happen anytime, anywhere.

But what about times when something happened against
the order "which we know" but it was not actually a miracle? What if the event really had a scientific explanation

---

1   St. Augustine, Contra Faustum, Book XXVI, no. 3, http://www
     .newadvent.org/fathers/140626.htm.

but, in the history of mankind, no one had discovered the physical explanation yet? What if the alleged miracle later had a scientific, natural explanation that was simply not well-understood at the time when it seemed like a miracle happened? Undoubtedly, that has been the case at times. As we shall see with Eucharistic miracles, alleged miracles in the Catholic Church are sometimes subjected to investigation to determine if a miracle happened. Even if a natural explanation is discovered later, the event that *seemed* against the order "which we know" in the moment would still technically qualify as a miracle. How can this be? It is because God knows what we know in those moments. He knows whether something will appear miraculous or not. The important thing about miracles is not that they are always beyond nature but that they are God communicating with us to show His love. After all, with God all things are possible.[2]

Some may disagree with this assessment, but any scientist can testify that our knowledge of the natural world is dwarfed by our ignorance of it. Our knowledge is incomplete. If a person's faith comes to depend on the scientific investigation of an alleged miraculous event—such as might be the case for someone who would not believe in the Real Presence of Christ in the Eucharist unless the Eucharistic miracles are proven true beyond doubt—that is not faith at all. The supernatural gift of faith is a gift that rests on our intellectual assent to the testimony of Jesus Christ. Before studying miracles, this point must be firmly in one's grasp. *Our faith does not depend on science.*

---

2   See Mt 19:26.

This subtle point is emphasized by St. Aquinas as he expounded on St. Augustine's words. In classical Latin, *mīrāculum* refers to an object of wonder. The word is derived from admiration when an event happens but its cause is hidden. Miracles cause us to be full of wonder because the cause is God who is hidden from us all. St. Aquinas defined a miracle as "those things which God does outside those causes which we know." Notice again that he kept the phrase "which we know" (or at least it was kept in translation). When we cover the Eucharistic miracles across time, take special note that increasingly, as our scientific understanding of the world has grown, the simple message of these miracles is that Christ is truly here and *present* with us, not just in mystical spiritual form, but really present, physically, in the Holy Eucharist.

Transubstantiation: A Miracle of Being

The word "transubstantiation" is unique to Catholicism, has one meaning, and therefore shares no synonyms. The word also has a history. Transubstantiation was codified in the sixteenth century by the Council of Trent (1546–1543). The council declared, just as Christ Himself first announced at the institution of the Eucharist, that it is truly His body offered "under the species" of bread and wine and that "by the consecration of the bread and of the wine, a conversion is made of the whole substance of the bread into the substance of the body of Christ our Lord, and of the whole substance of the wine into the substance of his blood; which conversion is, by the holy Catholic Church, suitably and properly called transubstantiation."[3]

The term was not new to the council, however. It was invented by theologians of the eleventh and twelfth centuries, in Latin *Transsubstantiatio* and *Transsubstantiare*.[4] The Latin form is noted as early as 1070 in St. Peter Damian's writings.[5] Pope Alexander III, who convoked the Third Lateran Council in 1179, used the term in 1150 in his writing before ascending the hierarchy to become pope. Pope Innocent III (1198) used it in his decretals. In 1215, the Fourth Lateran Council repeated the word in the Creed of canon 1. Invoking Aristotelian natural philosophy in the thirteenth century, St. Thomas Aquinas developed the concept in the *Summa Theologiae*.[6]

The term was codified in the Council of Trent in response to Martin Luther's doctrine of consubstantiation, which holds that the substances of bread and wine are joined together with the body and blood of Christ.[7] The prefix "con-" means "occurring together" whereas the prefix "trans-" means "change." The difference in the two words is the difference between heresy and truth. At the Last Supper, Christ said, "This is my body." He did not say, "Here in this bread is my body." Likewise, He said, "This is my blood," not "Here in this wine is my blood." The bread and wine do not join or unite with the body and blood, but rather the bread and wine are entirely and absolutely changed into the body and blood

---

3   The Fourth Lateran Council, Chapter IV; also CCC 1376.
4   Ludwig Ott, *Fundamentals of Catholic Dogma* (Charlotte: TAN Books, 1974), 379.
5   Peter Damian, *Expos. Canonis Missæ*, §7.
6   ST.III.75.
7   Ludwig Ott, *Fundamentals of Catholic Dogma*, 379.

of Christ, a conversion of the whole substance of the bread into the substance of the body of Christ and of the whole substance of the wine into the substance of His blood. This change is also unique in that as the substance changes, the appearances (the species) do not. The body appears as bread; the blood appears as wine.

Although the word is almost a millennium old, it still applies in the context of modern chemistry. Scholastics identified a *terminus a quo* and a *terminus ad quem*: that which ceases to be and that which begins to be. For creation out of nothing, there is a negative *terminus a quo*; that is, nothing is changed into something.[8] For annihilation, there is a negative *terminus ad quem*; something is changed into nothing. Transubstantiation, being without synonym, is not like either of these kinds of changes. Something (bread and wine) is changed into something (body and blood).

Modern chemistry has no analog for this kind of change since all substantial changes in chemistry involve the rearrangement of atomic bonds. For example, hydrogen gas and oxygen are individual substances. When they react, bonds are broken, and new ones formed so that water molecules have two hydrogens bonded to one oxygen. Chemistry certainly has no word for negative being since matter is conserved in chemical reactions. Humans neither create matter out of nothing nor destroy matter. The number of grams of reactants (the *terminus a quo*) equals the number of grams of products (*terminus ad quem*).

A Eucharistic miracle begins with the pre-existing matter of bread and wine, but no rearrangement of atoms and bonds occurs. The species of bread and wine become the

8 ST.III.75.3.

body and blood. Both have positive being. For transubstantiation, we say it like this: the whole substance of the bread and wine becomes the body and blood of Christ.[9] Matter is conserved, just as in chemical reactions. The type of conversion is different, however, and this requires another exploration of terminology. In nature, scholastics describe two kinds of conversions: accidental and substantial.

In an accidental conversion, the substance assumes a new appearance, such as when paper is folded, copper is drawn into wires, or ice melts. A modern chemist calls such a change of appearance a *physical* change. Paper, copper, water exist before the conversion. Paper, copper, water exist after, just in a new shape. At the atomic level, no bonds between atoms are broken and no bonds between atoms are reformed to make the products. The substance itself, therefore, does not change. Water is still water whether it is frozen solid, liquid, or gas.

In a substantial conversion, one form becomes another form. The matter is still there—such as when paper burns by combustion, copper oxidizes, or hydrogen and oxygen gas become water. But the matter becomes new substances. In modern chemistry, this is called a *chemical* change. The bonds between atoms break and new bonds form to make different compounds with different compositions and consequently *different properties*. Sodium metal is explosive. Chlorine gas is toxic. When a substance forms with a ratio of one sodium atom (in the form of Na^+ ion) to one chlorine atom (in the form of Cl^- ion), something called table salt forms which is neither explosive nor toxic. The difference is that the electrons orbiting the nuclei in the atoms changed

---

9   ST. III.75.4.

where they orbit, thereby binding the atoms together in a new way. It is a bit like playing with LEGO® blocks. A substantial conversion involves unsnapping atoms and re-snapping them back together into a new object.

In nature, both for the medieval populations and in chemistry for scientists today, we say that the new substances have unique properties. Ashes look nothing like paper, rust nothing like copper, water and salt nothing like explosive gases. Even if the reactants and products appear the same, as they sometimes do, an elemental analysis would show that the *composition* is in fact different. The atoms must regroup, or it is not a chemical reaction.

In nature, however, every substantial conversion (rearrangement of bonds) also causes an accidental conversion (change in physical and chemical properties). Here is where transubstantiation is different, and it is really a simple concept, so simple it can be taught to second grade students preparing for the sacrament of Holy Communion. The bread and wine become the body and blood of Christ but retain the appearance, taste, smell, and feel of bread and wine. As many a catechist knows, we say there is a substantial conversion but no accidental conversion. In transubstantiation, there is a change of substance but no change of physical appearance or property. No chemical bonds are broken and reformed. The new word was adopted precisely for this reason. Transubstantiation is a conversion to a new substance, but it is unlike any natural conversion. The form changes, but the physical properties do not. It literally comes down to faith in the words of Christ. "This is my body." *Our beautiful faith hinges on one two-letter word of being.*

After transubstantiation occurs, the atoms and molecules continue interacting according to the laws of nature, just as they are, completely unaffected, as if nothing miraculous had happened at all. There is no chemical reaction and no accompanying physical change. The consecration breaks no chemical bonds and synthesizes no new ones. But the substance is converted anyway! And that is the uniqueness even recognized and taught by the scholastics. "The mode of Christ's presence under the Eucharistic species is unique."[10] The whole substance—but only the substance—is converted. As Catholics, we literally kneel and stare at a wafer of bread and chalice of wine and believe with our hearts and minds that Christ becomes truly present at the consecration. It is the purest and simplest act of faith.

But what about time? It's one thing to accept that transubstantiation occurs. It is a different question altogether to ask *when* it occurs. Due to its uniqueness, transubstantiation cannot occur in steps. St. Thomas Aquinas pondered this question as well. He concluded that the bread and wine do not disappear in steps or by motion.[11] There are no intermediate states or successive changes like batter baking or grapes fermenting. The two species change in full form by pure being. And, yes, this is a mystery.

The best we can express with our human limitations is that transubstantiation occurs instantly. But what is an instant? Modern science deals with very tiny intervals of time down to the nanosecond (billionth of a second), picosecond (trillionth of a second), and femtosecond (quadrillionth of a second). However, in science, even an

10   CCC 1374.
11   ST.III.75.3.

infinitesimally small instant is taken to still be an interval in time. In physics, we speak of "instantaneous" rate. That is like when you glance at your speedometer in your car to gauge your speed at that instant, but time passes in the time it takes to move your eye to the speedometer and register the number in your brain. An instant in science is defined as a time interval that approaches zero, and that is as close as we can come to a timeless instant.

Transubstantiation, St. Aquinas says, occurs in a timeless instant. St. Aquinas expresses this change as both in becoming and in being simultaneously. This change, he says, is caused by a power that is infinite to which it belongs to operate in an instant, meaning that only God's infinite power could cause the whole substance to change beyond and outside of time because only God can instantly dispose matter to any form.

There is a similar concept in analytic geometry. An "asymptote" is a line on a graph that approaches nearer and nearer to a given curve but never intersects with it even out to infinity. It is kind of the same concept as when you try to walk half the distance across a room, and then half again, and then half again, and you realize you could infinitely keep halving the space while simultaneously being able to take ten steps and reach the other wall. As it relates to the Holy Eucharist, we can think of it like this: when the Eucharist unites us with the heavenly liturgy, we literally glimpse eternity, not with our eyes, but with our intellects and will.

Transubstantiation is the most logical formulation possible to articulate Christ's instructions at the Last Supper.

Faith is the substance of things unseen.[12] What could be more unseen than a substantial conversion that cannot be observed with the most precise elemental analysis? The Eucharistic belongs to the perfection of faith.[13]

Above all, transubstantiation happens because Christ, the Word who was in the beginning, said so. It is the simplest and deepest reality, and the reason that molecules, atoms, wheat, and grapevines, or any of us exist at all. Everything is what it is because God speaks it into existence and holds it there. During the Eucharistic Prayer, the celebrant raises the bread above the altar. He looks upward. He bows slightly. He says, "Take this, all of you, and eat of it, for this is my body, which will be given up for you." The altar bells ring, and right then and there the change occurs in front of us.

It would be irresponsible to embark on a serious discussion of Eucharistic miracles without these principles firmly grasped in our hearts and minds.

Eucharistic Miracles

We must, therefore, start out affirming that the Catholic does not need Eucharistic miracles to prove the Catholic faith. We take Christ, the Second Person of the Holy Trinity incarnate, the Word, at His *word*. He said the consecrated host is His body and the wine become His blood, so it is so. He comes to be with us physically in every Mass.

Eucharistic miracles occur when, in addition to transubstantiation, there is also a physical, chemical, and/or

12   See Heb 1:11.
13   ST.III.75.1.

MIRACLES AND TRANSUBSTANTIATION

biological substantial change where God does something against that order of nature which we know and are accustomed to observing.

In many cases, the consecrated Host is said to become human flesh, or the wine becomes human blood, but there are other instances where other physical changes occur that defy explanation, such as when consecrated Hosts are said to have survived rainfall, left indentations on stone, or caused animals to behave differently.

How can we trust that the Eucharistic miracle reports are true? That requires faith in the scientists and investigators. The Church has a process for investigating alleged miracles. If something happens outside the order "which we know," the local priest and congregation may make a report to their bishop. The bishop may then launch an investigation. He may consult with experts to decide which people to appoint to the investigation team, or he even may request that the Holy See take over the investigation. Alleged miracles are sometimes observed and analyzed for a long time. The investigators explore possible natural explanations for the phenomena. After the report is prepared, which can take nearly a decade, it is presented to the bishop, and the bishop decides whether to declare the miracle authentic. As the analytical capabilities in science decipher the data with greater precision, the investigations become more intense.

Nevertheless, Eucharistic miracles are considered private revelations, and Christians are not obligated to believe they occurred. This is not because we doubt that God could work such miracles, but it is because we can never be certain of the scientific investigation. Because we are free to doubt scientific findings, we are also free to decide whether

we think the miracle happened or not. We are not required
to accept even Church-approved miracles. We are free to
examine the evidence and make our own conclusions. To
reiterate, we cannot deny that miracles occur. Their possibility is a truth of faith, for Christ Himself worked many
miracles. Miracles are found throughout the Old and New
Testaments. The Church urges prudence in the determination of modern supernatural phenomena.

As we review the data from some of the Eucharistic miracles and discuss how to engage and defend the truths of
the Catholic faith, keep in mind that God, like the loving
father who brings gifts to his children even if it means sus-
pending all his usual rules, is still communicating with us.
He wants us to know and love Him. More than anything,
the Eucharist is about being in Christ's presence so we can
know and love Him more and serve Him better in this life.
We were not meant for this life alone, where science tells
us so much about the way nature works. Rather, we are
meant for eternal life in heaven with our Creator and our
Redeemer. We do not need Eucharistic miracles to believe
that God reaches out to us with all His heart at every Mass.

Review/Summary

Key Ideas

- When God works a miracle, He is making
  Himself known in a very personal way tailored
  to the individuals and the situations. He does not
  violate or change the rules of nature. Miracles
  go beyond nature.

- The term "transubstantiation" was codified in the Council of Trent in response to Martin Luther's doctrine of consubstantiation. The prefix "con-" means "occurring together" whereas the prefix "trans-" means "change." The difference in the two words is the difference between heresy and truth.
- Eucharistic miracles happen when, in addition to transubstantiation, there is also a physical, chemical, and biological substance change where God does something against that order of nature which we know and are accustomed to observing.

Good Facts to Memorize

- Transubstantiation happens because Christ, the Word who was in the beginning, said so. It is the simplest and deepest reality, the reason that molecules, atoms, wheat, and grapevines, or anything, or any of us, exists at all.

Effective Questions to Ask When Discussing the Real Presence

- Are miracles necessary?
- Is it necessary to believe miracles are possible?
- How do you know if you can believe Eucharistic miracles happened?
- What evidence would there need to be?
- Should faith depend on Eucharistic miracles?

10

THE FEAST OF CORPUS CHRISTI

Peter of Prague and Tradition

ACCORDING to tradition, a Eucharistic miracle occurred in the small Umbrian town of Bolsena, Italy, near Rome, in 1263.[1] A German priest known as Peter of Prague was travelling through Bolsena on his way to Rome.[2] He had embarked on such a long journey (from Prague to Rome) to strengthen his faith in the Eucharist and resolve his doubts about the transubstantiation of the bread and wine into the body and blood of Christ. The priest stopped to celebrate Holy Mass in the Church of St. Cristina, a usual resting place for pilgrims to Rome. St. Cristina was a woman of unwavering faith venerated as a Christian martyr from the third century.

Peter prayed with devotion at the tomb of St. Cristina. Then he celebrated Holy Mass there. After he spoke the words of consecration, this doubting Peter of Prague reported that blood issued from the Host as he held it above the chalice. He said the blood trickled down his hands and

---

1   "Il Miraculo Eucaristico," Basilica di S. Cristina, Santuario del Miracolo Eucaristico, http://www.basilicasantacristina.it/index.php/it/il-miracolo, accessed August 19, 2020.

2   "Pietro de Praga," Basilica di S. Cristina, Santuario del Miracolo Eucaristico, http://www.basilicasantacristina.it/index.php/it/pietro-di-praga, accessed August 19, 2020.

drenched the cloth known as the corporal (from Latin *cor-porālis*, "of the body") on the altar. Peter could not continue officiating the ceremony because he was so elated. He wrapped the Eucharist in the corporal and went to the sacristy. As he walked, drops of blood spilled onto the marble floor.

The people in the village of Bolsena spread the news of the miracle quickly and decided to form a procession to deliver the blood-stained cloth to a nearby city of Orvieto for Pope Urban IV to see. Orvieto is also near Rome, and this is where the pope lived. The pope heard about the miracle from the clergymen who accompanied Peter of Prague and the people of the village.

The pope is said to have been so excited that he gathered Church dignitaries, such as archbishops and cardinals, to meet the procession on the bridge at Rio Chiaro and welcome them. Before the large crowd that followed, Pope Urban IV kneeled and received the miraculous Host and blood-stained corporal. When Peter met with Pope Urban IV, he confessed his doubt and received absolution.

Pope Urban IV appointed representatives from his court to investigate the alleged miracle at Bolsena. Among these representatives was the bishop of Orvieto, Giacomo Mala-traga. He was accompanied by the theologians Thomas Aquinas and Bonaventure from Bagnoregio. They were to ascertain the facts of the case and bring all the relics from the miracle back to Orvieto.

The pope placed the relics in the Cathedral of Orvieto, where they are still enshrined today. The Basilica of St. Cristina in Bolsena remains her tomb, and the altar upon which the miracle occurred resides in a new chapel built in 1693.

Pope Urban IV is credited with instituting the feast of Corpus Christi (Body of Christ) throughout the Latin rite with the publication of his papal bull *Transiturus de hoc mundo*. There is disagreement among scholars as to the connection between this miracle and this solemn commemoration throughout the universal Church.[3] The bull was issued in 1264, one year after the miracle was reported.

St. Thomas Aquinas contributed to both the bull and the liturgical works. The shortest narrative holds that Pope Urban IV was "prompted" by the Eucharistic miracle to institute the feast day and that he commissioned Thomas Aquinas to compose the Office for the Mass and Liturgy of the Hours to honor the Holy Eucharist as the Body of Christ.[4] Historians have provided a broader context of this period during the High Middle Ages (1000–1347) in Italy, and we find some inconsistencies in the story.

Inconsistencies in the History

Corpus Christi liturgies already existed nearly two decades before the papal bull extended the solemnity to the universal Church. Evangelical movements in southern France

---

3   Volumen V, Tomus I: *Acta Urbani IV, Clementis IV, Gregorii X* (1261-1276) (Typis Polyglottis Vaticanis, 1953), pp. 43–47.

4   Joan Carroll Cruz, *Eucharistic Miracles and the Eucharistic Phenomena in the Lives of the Saints* (Charlotte: TAN Books, 1987), 64. *Catalogue of the Vatican International Exhibition: The Eucharistic Miracles of the World*, Presented by the Real Presence Eucharistic Education and Adoration Association, Inc. (Bardstown: Eternal Life, 2016), 114–117.

and northern Italy had produced heretical ideas that denied the Eucharist as a sacrament.[5] In response, intense devotion to the Eucharist arose among the laity, especially women. The center of the Eucharistic movement was further north in Liège, Belgium.[6] During this time, actions still practiced today became popular, such as the practices of reserving the Blessed Sacrament in the tabernacle, displaying the host on the altar for adoration, and ringing bells at the elevation of the Eucharist during Mass.[7]

In 1246, the bishop of Liège, Robert of Torote, authorized a special feast day on the first Thursday after Trinity Sunday to commemorate the institution of the Holy Eucharist by the Lord. The purpose was to establish a special day outside of Lent, and all its sorrow, to celebrate a feast more solemn and joyful. A liturgy was then composed for the Diocese of Liège.[8] In 1252, the feast spread to Germany as well.

Jacques Pantaléon, elected as Pope Urban IV in 1261, witnessed the solemnities in Liège and knew the people responsible for it. He was probably petitioned to make the feast universal long before the report of a miracle from Bolsena. Further, St. Thomas Aquinas would not have composed a liturgy from its very beginning. He would have combined chosen elements from Scripture, Tradition, and *existing* liturgies and then added new hymns and prayers to articulate the theological and devotional aspects of the Church.

Some historians have not only questioned the link of Pope Urban IV's institution of the feast of Corpus Christi

---

5   James A. Weisheipl, *Friar Thomas D'Aquino: His Life, Thought, and Work* (Garden City: Doubleday, 1974), 178.

6   Ibid.

7   Ibid.

8   Ibid.

to the Eucharistic miracle at Bolsena, but they are also skeptical that the miracle even happened. Miri Rubin, historian and professor of medieval and early modern history and author of the 452-page *Corpus Christi: The Eucharist in Late Medieval Culture*, concludes that the attempt to link the founding of the feast to the Bolsena miracle seems to be "misplaced."[9] The author notes that this was the first time a universal feast was instituted by a pope, and as such, there pre-existed no quick procedure to undertake a sweeping institution of a new universal feast only one year after the alleged miracle.

The language in *Transiturus*, however, is remarkable for echoing the longstanding devotion Pope Urban IV had to the Holy Eucharist in the decades prior. The pope does not mention the miracle in the papal bull at all, nor does St. Thomas Aquinas in his liturgical writings. Rubin argues that Pope Urban IV's actions are more consistent with the social climate playing out over decades in northern Italy and further north in Liège where the pope had many connections. Further, Rubin points out that the date of the miracle is not known. Both inconsistencies lead Rubin to conclude that the miracle did not really occur.

Furthermore, the *Catholic Encyclopedia* article on "Orvieto" written in 1911 by Fr. Umberto Benigni, an Italian ecclesiastical historian, states that the "Miracle of Bolsena is not supported by strong historical evidence, and its tradition is not altogether consistent."[10] In addition to the pope making no mention of it in the papal bull by which he

---

9   Miri Rubin, *Corpus Christi: The Eucharist in Late Medieval Culture*, 1st Edition (Cambridge: Cambridge University Press, 1991), 176.

10   Umberto Benigni, "Orvieto," *The Catholic Encyclopedia* (New York: Robert Appleton Company, 1911).

established the feast of Corpus Christi, two biographers of Pope Urban IV likewise do not mention the miracle. They do, however, detail his acts as pontiff, including his stay at Orvieto and his devotion to the body of Christ.[11] It seems they would have mentioned the miracle if the pope had gone to such measures as organizing a party of dignitaries to meet Peter of Prague on the bridge at Rio Chiaro and then ordering a new universal feast day.

Pope Urban IV died in the same year the miracle was reported, in October of 1264, having left nothing in writing about the miracle. A quarter of a century later, a *sacra rappresentazione* (holy performance, sacred oration) dated between the 1290s and 1344 records the miracle.[12] The histories are inscribed in the enamel of the reliquary in the Church of St. Cristina in Bolsena around 1337–1339, and they too mention the miracle.[13] A play based on the miracle was popularized around this time and is performed every year in the town of Orvieto.

In 1344, Pope Urban IV's successor, Pope Clement VI, gives a short account of the miracle in a brief.[14] The sermons of Dominican preacher Leonardo Mattei of Udine in 1435 and the chronicles compiled by St. Antoninus of Florence in 1459 frequently reference the miracle, and the latter

---

11   These are listed in the Catholic Encyclopedia article, "Muratori, *Rerum Italicarum scriptores*, III, pt. l, 400 sq.; and especially Thierricus Vallicoloris."

12   Kristen Van Ausdall, "Art and Eucharist in the Late Middle Ages," in *A Companion to the Eucharist in the Middle Ages*, ed. Ian Levy, Gary Macy, Kristen Van Ausdall (Leiden, Boston: Brill, 2012), 584, footnote 89.

13   Umberto Benigni, "Orvieto."

14   Ibid.

even mentions a German priest on pilgrimage to Rome with doubts about the Real Presence of Christ in the Eucharist.[15]

The account provided on the Basilica of St. Cristina website says the popular tradition was handed down through both iconographic and literary sources.[16] Additionally, the basilica in Bolsena and cathedral in Orvieto house the relics from the miracle still today. The miraculous Host, the corporal stained with blood (the Corporal of Bolsena), and the cloths used to wipe the chalice and paten are kept in the Cathedral of Orvieto. These were enshrined in gold since 1337. The altar and marble slabs stained with blood remain in Bolsena.

Most famously, a painting by the Italian renaissance artist Raphael produced between 1512 and 1514 adorns the Raphael Rooms in the Apostolic Palace at the Vatican. Titled *The Mass at Bolsena*, the painting shows the priest celebrating Mass with the bleeding Host and a stained cloth on the altar with Pope Julius II (1443–1513) kneeling at the altar.

Every year in Bolsena and Orvieto, the Solemnity of the Feast of Corpus Christi is celebrated with a great procession. In 1964, the seven hundredth anniversary of the miracle, Pope Paul VI celebrated Holy Mass at the altar where the Corporal of Bolsena is kept.[17]

The inconsistencies surrounding this Eucharistic miracle are instructional for any student of history. We are left to combine fragments of the story based on the testimony of others who themselves accepted the story as tradition. There is no way to go back in time and acquire direct knowledge

15 Ibid. James A. Weisheipl, *Friar Thomas D'Aquino*, 179.

16 "Il Miraculo Eucaristico," Basilica di S. Cristina, Santuario del Miracolo Eucaristico.

17 Joan Carroll Cruz, *Eucharistic Miracles and the Eucharistic Phenomena in the Lives of the Saints*, 64.

of the event. The strength of the evidence comes from the consistencies that can be found.

Catholics are not obligated to accept this miracle as truth, but since this miracle is approved, we are permitted to believe a traveling German priest actually witnessed a bleeding Host and notified the pope. And perhaps the Bolsena and Orvieto citizens were so moved by this event that their fervor led Pope Urban IV to extend the already established feast to the entire Church so that still today we all celebrate the feast of Corpus Christi on the first Thursday after the octave of Pentecost throughout the world.

Review/Summary

Key Ideas

- According to tradition, a Eucharistic miracle occurred in Bolsena, Italy in 1263 when a German priest celebrated Holy Mass. Blood issued from the Host, drenched the corporal, and spilled onto the marble floor. Pope Urban IV is said to have initiated an investigation due to his excitement.
- Pope Urban IV is also credited for instituting the feast of Corpus Christi, but there is disagreement as to the connection between this miracle and the solemn commemoration throughout the universal Church.
- Some historians have not only questioned the link between Pope Urban IV's instituting the feast of Corpus Christi and the Eucharistic miracle at Bolsena, but they are also skeptical that the miracle even happened.

Good Facts to Memorize

- The feast of Corpus Christi was the first time a universal feast was instituted by a pope.
- The miraculous Host, the corporal stained with blood (the Corporal of Bolsena), and the cloths used to wipe the chalice and paten are kept in the Cathedral of Orvieto. These were enshrined in gold since 1337.
- Every year in Bolsena and Orvieto, the Solemnity of the Feast of Corpus Christi is celebrated with a great procession.
- In 1964, the seven hundredth anniversary of the miracle, Pope Paul VI celebrated Holy Mass at the altar where the Corporal of Bolsena is kept.
- Today we celebrate the feast of Corpus Christi on the first Thursday after the octave of Pentecost throughout the world.

Effective Questions to Ask When Discussing the Real Presence

- What standards of proof are appropriate when ascertaining the veracity of alleged miracles?
- Why does the Church not require Catholics to accept the reports of Eucharistic miracles as true?
- How might one form a reasonable conclusion about the Eucharistic miracle that is said to have been tied to the feast of Corpus Christi?

11

THE BUENOS AIRES MIRACLES

Four Events in the 1990s

IN the 1990s, four Eucharistic miracles were reported in Buenos Aires, Argentina—two in 1992, another in 1994, and another in 1996—all at the same parish of Santa Maria on Avenue la Plata. Only the alleged miracle in 1996 was investigated scientifically.

In the first case, on May 1, 1992, a layman and extraordinary minister of Holy Communion, Carlos Dominguez, went to reserve the Blessed Sacrament and found two pieces of the consecrated Host in the shape of a half-moon on the corporal.[1] Carlos took the pieces to the priest. Father Juan Salvador Carlomagno placed the fragments in water and stored them in the tabernacle.

---

1   Institute of St. Clement I, *The Eucharistic Miracles of the World (I Miracoli Eucaristici nel mondo. Catalogo della mostra internazionale.)* (Bardstown, KY: Eternal Life, 2016), p. 2; and Ary Waldir Ramos Diaz, "The future Pope Francis was in charge of dealing with this reported Eucharistic miracle," *Aleteia*, June 6, 2020, https://aleteia .org/2020/06/13/the-future-pope-francis-was-in-charge-of-dealing -with-this-reported-eucharistic-miracle/.

To understand what happened, some terminology and norms of the Catholic Church need to be reviewed. The corporal (from Latin *corporālis*, "of the body") is the cloth on the altar that the paten, chalice, and ciborium are set upon during the celebration of the Mass. The paten is the small plate that holds the bread (host) and holy body of Christ. The chalice is the drinking vessel that holds the wine and holy blood of Christ. The ciborium is the covered vessel that holds the consecrated Hosts for distribution of Holy Communion to the laity.

The *Catechism of the Catholic Church* affirms that during Mass, the Eucharistic presence of Christ begins at the moment of the consecration and endures as long as the Eucharistic species subsist (CCC 1377). Christ is present "whole and entire" in every fragment of the consecrated Host. The breaking of the bread does not divide Christ. Therefore, Christ is present whole and entire in a fragment that falls onto the corporal or that even falls by mistake to the floor. As such, there is a procedure for disposing of fragments that are not consumed.

The sacristy of each church is the room where sacred vessels and vestments are kept. In the sacristy, there is a sacrarium. This is a sink that drains directly into the ground and bypasses the sewer system. The purpose of the sacrarium is to prevent holy water or any water with dissolved consecrated Hosts from being profaned by being dumped into the sewer. Through the sacrarium, they go straight back to the earth. The proper way to dispose of any consecrated Host, which is the body of Christ, is to place it in water and allow it to dissolve. Once the species is no longer visibly intact, the solution is poured down the sacrarium.

Because Catholics believe that Christ is truly present in the Holy Eucharist, they treat all of it, even fragments, with reverence.

Hence it was, according to procedure, that the half-moon-shaped consecrated Host under the protection of Father Carlomagno was placed in water in the tabernacle to dissolve. On May 8, 1992, a week after the fragments were stored in water, Father Carlomagno says that he observed a red color on the Host and in the surrounding water when he checked on the fragment.[2]

On May 10, a few days later, more than one drop of a red substance was also found on the patens during two evening Masses, accounting for a second alleged miracle in a few weeks.[3] Father Carlomagno also said that three blood clots had formed in the water where the first consecrated Host fragment was stored, and he said, alarmingly, that blood was also on the walls of the tabernacle, as if the Host had exploded.[4] So there was a red substance in the tabernacle where the Host fragment was stored and new appearance of a red substance on the patens during Mass.

At the same location, a third miracle was alleged a few years later, on July 24, 1994, during a Sunday children's Mass. A Eucharistic minister saw a drop of a red substance dripping along the side of a pix. A pix is a small disc-shaped container that holds consecrated Hosts while the priest or extraordinary minister distributes the body of Christ to the faithful.

---

2   Ary Waldir Ramos Diaz, "The future Pope Francis was in charge of dealing with this reported Eucharistic miracle."

3   Institute of St. Clement I, *The Eucharistic Miracles of the World*, p. 2.

4   Ary Waldir Ramos Diaz, "The future Pope Francis was in charge of dealing with this reported Eucharistic miracle."

Then again, a few years later on August 15, 1996, during the Mass of the Solemnity of the Assumption of the Blessed Virgin Mary, a seventy-seven-year-old woman named Emma Fernandez reported that near the end of the distribution of Holy Communion, a woman came up to her and told her that a consecrated Host was abandoned in a candle holder on the far side of the church.[5] This, of course, would be a very serious matter. The two women went to the candle holder, found the consecrated Host, and showed it to Father Alejandro Pezet, the priest who had celebrated the evening Mass.

Father Pezet said in an interview that the candle holder was not used much.[6] He said that he picked the Host up with his fingers and took it to the altar to consume it but, noticing how dirty the Host was, instead instructed Emma Fernandez to follow the procedure for dissolving the Host so it could be disposed of in the sacrarium—that is, to put it in a bowl of water and place it in the tabernacle, like had been done in 1992.

Eleven days later, on August 26, Emma unlocked the tabernacle and observed that the Host exuded a red substance that looked like fresh human blood. Emma told Father Pezet and another priest, Father Eduardo Graham.

The account says that the authorities were informed about this event and a professional photographer, Marcelo Antonini, was commissioned to record the changes. The Host was mostly undissolved and still had a circular shape. The edges were no longer crisp but in the process of dissolving.

5   Ron Tesoriero and Lee Han, *Unseen: The Origin of Life Under the Microscope*, (Kincumber: Tesoriero, 2013), 44.
6   Ibid., 43.

Dark spots surrounded by red liquid were also in the bowl over the Host, appearing to emerge (exude) from it.[7]

Father Pezet then moved the bowl with the transformed Host from the public tabernacle in the church to a private tabernacle in the presbytery, which is the part of a church reserved for the officiating clergy. Three priests, Fathers Pezet, Graham, and Juan Carlomagna had the key for access to the tabernacle. Over the next few weeks, Father Pezet said that more of the red substance appeared and that the Host was only in the custody of the priests who had access to the presbyteral tabernacle.

By September 6, over three weeks since it was found dirty and abandoned in the candle holder, dark globular masses that looked like coagulated blood had formed and the red liquid began to turn brownish. A month later, in October, the coagulated contents, but not the red liquid, were moved to distilled water and stored in a sterilized test tube, where they remained at Santa Maria Church for three years.

The Leukocyte Formula in 1992

Although no scientific investigation was performed on the 1992 or 1994 specimen, there was a single report of a blood test on the 1992 event. Volunteer investigator Ricardo Castañon Gomez reported seven years later in 1999 that the blood analysis "presented the entire leukocyte formula."[8] He was referring to a test performed by a parishioner, a woman who was a chemist. "Everyone knows," Castañon

---

7   Ibid., 46–47.

8   Institute of St. Clement I, *The Eucharistic Miracles of the World*, p. 3.

Gomez said, "that when one draws blood it is possible to obtain the leukocyte formula."

The chemist said that the sample was human blood and that she was surprised to observe that the "white blood cells were active." White blood cells are known to be stable one to two days in microscope samples without any preparation.[9] Depending on the time elapsed before the chemist ran the test, active white blood cells may be remarkable because their presence may then indicate that the blood came from a living human.

This claim, then, merits an examination. In his testimony, Castañon Gomez is talking to priests who are recounting the report of a chemist who ran a test years prior. The "leukocyte formula" and "active white blood cells" refer to the white blood cell count in human blood. Typically, in a routine medical exam, or if there is a condition suspected that affects the blood, a complete blood count (CBC) is done. The white blood cell count (WBC) is part of the complete test. The CBC gives the counts of red blood cells, white blood cells, and platelets. Other information is given about hemoglobin, volume percentage, size of cells, and for the white blood cells, the different types are counted. The five types of white blood cells are neutrophils, lymphocytes, monocytes, eosinophils, and basophils (some abnormal cells may also be present). These results are compared to references, looking for normal, high, or low levels. That is likely what the chemist and Castañon Gomez meant by

9   Douglas Palmer et al., "Flow cytometric determination of residual white blood cell levels in preserved samples from leukoreduced blood products," *Transfusion* Vol. 48 (January 2008), p. 198, https://doi.org/10.1111/j.1537-2995.2007.01489.x.

saying, "Everyone knows that when one draws blood it is possible to obtain the leukocyte formula."

The claim is confusing, though. If this is what is meant by leukocyte formula, it is not clear, nor is it explained, why the rest of the data was not reported. Perhaps no one at the time thought to preserve the data. White blood cell percentages are measured using either a microscope to manually count the cell types on a blood smear or by using an automated analyzer. These analyzers have been around since the 1950s. Early instruments used electricity to differentiate size and separately count red (smaller) and white (larger) blood cells. In the 1970s, new techniques of digital imaging and light scattering were developed. So it is likely the chemist had access to such an instrument and could have reported on a full blood count.

There are other concerns: Especially for the white blood cells, precautions must be taken with anticoagulants to prevent clumping, which would skew the data. It is baffling, then, for only a leukocyte formula to be reported in the absence of information about red blood cells or preparatory cautions taken on an atypical sample suspected of having a miraculous origin. In a more specific test, red blood cells can be lysed (broken) so that white blood cells are isolated and measured. If that was the only test performed, there should be an explanation for the decision not to measure red blood cells.

A leukocyte formula alone would only be a reading that gives information about the size of particles, coagulated or otherwise, in a sample. The priests also said the chemist reported that the white blood cells were active. This usually refers to size. Reactive lymphocytes show up as very large in a blood count. At a minimum, an analysis should have some consideration for the sample being something other than as assumed—that is, something other than human blood since the main question at hand was indeed whether the sample was human blood or not.

Nevertheless, according to the priests, no genetic tests were done at the time because of their complex nature. Castañon Gomez became one of the main proponents of the Buenos Aires allegations of miracles, and he was involved in the investigation of the 1996 sample as well.

The Investigation of the 1996 Sample

It is said that the custodian of the material in Buenos Aires requested an investigation, presumably around 1999.[10] No information is provided to explain what prompted the investigation nor why a more thorough investigation was not conducted on the three other events in 1992 and 1994. Interestingly, Pope Francis enters the story here, and it is helpful to backtrack and review how then bishop Jorge Mario Bergoglio played a role leading up to this Eucharistic investigation.

In May of 1992, Pope John Paul II had appointed Jorge Mario Bergoglio as titular bishop of Auca and auxiliary of Buenos Aires. He was appointed to this position because the current archbishop of Buenos Aires, Cardinal Antonio Quarracino, wanted Bergoglio as a collaborator. Bergoglio, who had studied chemistry, probably could have influenced

---

10   Ron Tesoriero and Lee Han, *Unseen: The Origin of Life Under the Microscope*, 43.

the commencement of an investigation of the 1992 alleged miracle.[11]

By the end of 1993, Bergoglio was appointed vicar general of the Archdiocese of Buenos Aires. In 1997, he was raised to coadjutor archbishop of Buenos Aires, and nine months later following the death of Cardinal Quarracino, Bergoglio succeeded him in February of 1998 as archbishop of Buenos Aires.

So it is, then, that the archbishop of Buenos Aires in 1999, who would later become Pope Francis, appointed Castañon Gomez as the lead scientist of the investigation of only the last, the 1996, alleged miracle. Castañon Gomez is a renowned clinical psychologist and president of the International Group for Peace (Grupo International para Paz). He also says that he was previously an atheist.

The nature of the investigation is curious, however. Another account says a decision was made to wait three years before beginning the investigation, but again, no explanation or reason is given for this delay.[12] Castañon Gomez said that he was appointed by the archbishop, but he was also working with documentary-makers Mike Willesee and Ron Tesoriero from Australia at the time. Willesee was an internationally known and accomplished journalist and, like Castañon Gomez, he was an atheist, except Willesee had not converted. Tesoriero was a lawyer who also served as the notary to verify the chain of custody for the samples upon the commencement of the investigation. It is not

---

11 "Biography of the Holy Father Francis," *L'Osservatore Romano*, Year LXIII, number 12 (Vatican), http://www.vatican.va/content/francesco /en/biography/documents/papa-francesco-biografia-bergoglio .html.

12 Institute of St. Clement I, *The Eucharistic Miracles of the World*, p. 3.

clear whether Ricardo Castañon Gomez along with Ron Tesoriero and Mike Willesee asked Archbishop Bergoglio to order an investigation or whether the request originated in the Church.

It seems that the former is the case. Castañon Gomez was already affiliated with Tesoriero and Willesee, as in 1995-1996 the team had produced a documentary, titled *The Stones Will Cry Out*, about a miracle in Bolivia in which a statue of Christ allegedly shed tears of blood that dried and left scabs.[13] Then again in 1998, the team produced another documentary titled *A Plea to Humanity* about a woman, also in Bolivia, named Katya Rivas who claimed that she suffered with Christ in His crucifixion with wounds on her hands, feet, and forehead, termed "the stigmata."[14] These were part of a longer documentary hosted by Willesee, *Science Tests Faith*, which aired in 1998.

At any rate, setting the uncertainty about the timing and the origin of the investigation aside, the team was only to investigate the event of 1996 in Buenos Aires.[15] Castañon Gomez said he told the archbishop he would conduct the scientific investigation at no cost. Eight scientists on four different continents—Australia, South America, North America, and Europe—were involved.

Castañon Gomez conducted interviews at the parish of Santa Maria, including the before mentioned testimony

---

13 Ron Tesoriero, *The Stones Will Cry Out*, Reason to Believe, https://reasontobelieve.com.au/the-stones-will-cry-out/.

14 Ron Tesoriero, *A Plea to Humanity*, Reason to Believe, https://reasontobelieve.com.au/a-plea-to-humanity/.

15 Ricardo Castañón Gomez, "Faith & Science Conference part II - Ricardo Castañon Ph.D.," San Migeulillo, Talk at the Faith and Science Conference, Mexico City, https://vimeo.com/5205626.

of the 1992 sample. Here is what he reported of the 1996 event. "On August 15, 1996, a faithful received the consecrated Host in his hands to take communion but he let it inadvertently fall to the ground and thought not to pick it up because it seemed 'dirty' to him. Another person, more pious, noticed what had happened, picked it up and placed it apart immediately informing the priest, Father Alejandro Pezet. The priest, following the directives of the Church in these circumstances, put the Host in a vessel full of water which he placed in the tabernacle awaiting that it would dissolve."[16]

This version of the story is materially different from the one told by Emma Fernandez, who was told by another woman that the Host was in a candle holder, so it is not clear how many different people touched the Host before it was stored in the tabernacle and then a test tube for three years. As will be discussed later, this has consequences on how the tests are interpreted.

Castañon Gomez also recorded interviews with five priests who were all witnesses of both the 1996 and the previous events in 1994 and 1992. Castañon Gomez said he was concerned that the priests had put the Host in water not because there was any problem with obeying procedural norms but because storage in water is the worst way to preserve a sample of blood or human tissue. His point was that even though procedural norms dictate dissolution in water for proper disposal, a biologist or forensic pathologist would have made a different choice. Had the priest expected biological material to form and had the priest wished to preserve it for analysis, water would be the worst storage medium. It would,

16   Institute of St. Clement I, *The Eucharistic Miracles of the World*, p. 3.

therefore, be miraculous that a biological sample could even remain intact in water for so long.

Problematic Forensic Genetic Testing

On October 21, 1999, the investigative journalism team sent the 1996 sample to the Forensic Analytical genetic laboratory in San Francisco. The results came back five months later, in May of 2000, and with some interesting results. Tesoriero, Willesse, and Castañon Gomez interpreted the report to say that the lab found fragments of human DNA in the samples and that the sample was human blood that contained the human genetic code. Tesoriero made this remarkable analytical report available in his book *Unseen: The Origin of Life Under the Microscope*.[17] This report bears examination.

The sample was first examined visually. The report recorded the presence of a coagulated substance, reddish-brown in color, in a clear liquid (water). Under a microscope, the red substance appeared attached to whitish fibrous material with no identifiable characteristics. When the sample dried, it was dark brown and particulate, as might be expected of blood.

The brown particles were then submitted to two kinds of routine forensic testing. Usually with a sample that appears to be biological in nature, a *presumptive* test is performed. In forensic science, a presumptive test begins with an underlying assumption about what the sample might be. For example, these initial quick and easy tests could

---

17   Ron Tesoriero and Lee Han, Unseen: *The Origin of Life Under the Microscope*, 246.

determine if a sample suspected to be blood or urine is not, in fact, one of those substances. More tests, called confirmatory tests, are needed to positively determine the identity of a substance.

The presumptive test used by the forensic lab on the Buenos Aires 1996 sample was a chemical ortho-tolidine test. In this test, a paper strip is infused with enzymes and a dye. The enzymes cause the conversion of glucose found in biological material to a chemical that reacts with the dye. The investigator can know in a matter of minutes, and with minimum equipment, if a sample contains glucose, which is a strong indication it might be biological.

The ortho-tolidine test on the brown particles was *negative*. However, this result does not necessarily prove the sample is not biological. The test only shows that the sample does *not* contain glucose. Glucose obtained from unprocessed blood samples has been shown to decrease by the hour due to glycolysis, so a sample that is three years old may not have any glucose to measure.[18] There is no explanation of any further tests to investigate whether the sample was actually blood, so this test is inconclusive.

About a third of the sample was prepared for a genetic test called PCR STR analysis. The acronym PCR STR stands for polymerase chain reaction, short tandem repeat. This is a common DNA profiling test for criminal investigations.[19]

---

18 Michael Turchiano et al., "Impact of Blood Sample Collection and Processing Methods on Glucose Levels in Community Outreach Studies," *Journal of Environmental and Public Health* (January 2013), https://doi.org/10.1155/2013/256151.

19 "What is STR Analysis?" National Institute of Justice (March 2, 2011), https://nij.ojp.gov/topics/articles/what-str-analysis.

To understand the results, a brief review of genetics and sample preparation is in order.

Among humans, nearly 99 percent of our DNA has mostly the same sequences. What differentiates each of us biologically as individuals is that the unique combination from our mother and father give us some DNA sequences that code for the proteins that make our physical traits such as hair and eye color, skin type, height, and a million other details.

The last 1 percent of DNA comprises millions of extra DNA units that do not code for any proteins at all. In these regions, scientists have discovered that there are multiple copies of short repeating sequences (the STR in the name of the test), usually two to seven base pairs long, termed short repeating tandem sequences. The number of repeats varies among individuals, such that they literally comprise a genetic fingerprint. The chance of two people having the exact same STR sequences throughout their genome is very small, though not impossible. A test that can measure these STR sequences provides nearly certain evidence that DNA found at a crime scene matches the DNA of a specific person in samples taken from tissues and fluids.

To prepare a sample for a PCR STR test, a special solvent is used to dissolve the DNA, if there is any, and separate it from the other material. The QuantiBlot® method, a human DNA quantification kit, was used for the test on the 1996 sample. It works by immobilizing the extracted DNA to a nylon membrane and then adding a molecular probe, specific to primates, to each strand. The probe interacts with light, so if primate DNA is present, the amount of it can be estimated by visually comparing test samples to standards of known DNA concentration. These tests take only a few hours and can measure very minute quantities, 0.15 ng to 10 ng of human or primate DNA.[20] For the 1996 sample, the San Francisco genetic forensic lab report only says that some substance was in the extractant but not enough for the DNA test to register a concentration, which would typically indicate there was not enough DNA for genetic analysis or that the test, being specific for primates, did not detect anything specific to that probe. Like the ortho-tolidine test, this genetic test is also inconclusive.

In general, it is not clear why these two forensic tests were chosen, aside from the fact that they are routine. Neither the ortho-tolidine nor the PCR STR tests are equipped to verify the allegation of a miraculous conversion of the consecrated Host into blood.

The presumptive ortho-tolidine test would not prove useful unless it were already verified that the three-year-old sample was miraculously *fresh blood* and the presence of glucose therefore expected. This seems an outrageous presumption if the point of the test is to provide evidence that a miracle occurred.

The PCR STR test is intended to *compare* the DNA of different humans. It is confirmatory in the sense that DNA on a piece of evidence can be confirmed to belong to, for example, the suspect in question (like matching fingerprints). But in the case of the Buenos Aires 1996 sample, there is no sample for comparison. This kind of test would only make sense if there were an actual known sample of Christ's blood for comparison.

---

20 Product Bulletin, QuantiBlot® Human DNA Quantitation Kit from Applied Biosystems, https://assets.thermofisher.com/TFS-Assets/LSG/manuals/cms_040281.pdf.

There is another concern regarding the amplification aspect of the PCR STR. Both accounts of the event
acknowledge that the Host was handled by several people.
Since the test is looking for only a small percentage (less
than 1 percent) of the DNA, a chemical step is needed to
amplify the STR segments. This amplification is done by
the widely used polymerase chain reaction (PCR) invented
in 1984.[21] It works as follows. 1) The DNA double strand in
solution is broken into two single strands (denatured) with
heat. 2) Then the temperature is lowered so that short segments of DNA, called primers, can find the STRs. These
primers have the complementary sequence for the known
loci (segments of DNA) that are found in the repeating
sections, so they go searching for the repeating segments.
3) Once discovered by the primers, nucleic acids also in
the solution synthesize the complementary strand, thereby
making a new double stranded DNA of just that segment.
As the temperature cycles high and low, the solution of
DNA, enzymes, primers, nucleic acids, and buffers continues to synthesize the STRs exponentially until there is
enough for the genetic "fingerprint" to be analyzed, in this
case by the QuantiBlot® method.

The most serious limitation of PCR STR analysis is precisely in its advantage—*very small amounts of DNA can
unintentionally be amplified.*[22] Even the smallest amount of

21   Randall Saiki et al., "Enzymatic Amplification of β -Globin Genomic
     Sequences and Restriction Site Analysis for Diagnosis of Sickle Cell
     Anemia," *Science*, Volume 230, Issue 4732 (December 1985), pp.
     1350–1354.
22   Gerald Schochetman et al., "Polymerase Chain Reaction," *The Jour-
     nal of Infectious Diseases*, Volume 158, Issue 6 (December 1988),
     pp. 1154–1157, https://doi.org/10.1093/infdis/158.6.1154.

DNA from multiple humans can be amplified together. If, for example, there are fingerprints on a specimen, the DNA of the person who made the fingerprints will be amplified along with the DNA in the sample, and the results will not be specific to a single individual.

For this reason, the analysis is typically done under controlled conditions in the laboratory, and sample handling prior to its arrival at the forensic lab is extremely important. Additionally, there is a problem if other matter from the environment is present. Humic substances, the products of organic matter decomposing in soil, can also inhibit PCR amplification.[23] New ways to solve this problem have been developed since at least 2015, but that is well after the time these samples were tested.

The testimony of witnesses is clear that the Host was touched multiple times: when the preparations were made for Mass, when the priest held it, when the person who placed it in the candle holder touched it, when the priest touched it again to carry it back to the altar, and when Emma Fernandez placed it in the bowl of water. The priest even said the Host was "very dirty" and we know the sample had been stored, presumably still dirty, in tap water for a couple of months before being stored in a test tube for three years and transferred to the forensic laboratory for five more months. Certainly, there could have been residual DNA from being held by multiple people, and there could have been contaminants from the dirt, both factors

---

23   Tao Geng and Richard Mathies, "Minimizing inhibition of PCR-STR typing using digital agarose droplet microfluidics," *Forensic Science International: Genetics*, Volume 14 (January 2015), pp. 203-209, https://doi.org/10.1016/j.fsigen.2014.10.007.

known to render a PCR STR analysis inconclusive. None of these concerns were addressed by the investigative team.

The test used by Forensic Analytical for the Buenos Aires 1996 red substance that formed on the consecrated Host was designed to specifically identify and amplify nine STR segments known to be found in humans. The test presumes that a sample originates from a human.

The report from May of 2000 on the 1996 alleged Eucharistic miracle says a small amount of human DNA was extracted from the sample but not enough to produce any amplified DNA for any of the nine STR loci. The Forensic Analytical lab therefore reported that no blood was detected in the sample (from the ortho-tolidine test) and that there may have been some DNA but not enough for successful STR analysis. Contamination might account for this observation, but again, the report does not address this possibility. Per routine forensic analysis, the sample was simply reported as non-biological material with possible DNA contamination and a "NR" for "no results" on the PCR STR test.

Tesoriero interprets this quite differently in his book. He claims that the Forensic Analytical report from May 1, 2000 *does* describe the presence of human DNA (because of the extractant) and that the sample may not be of human origin presumably on the basis that the tests failed to produce a human genetic profile.[24] Tesoriero interprets the results as miraculous.

"The results from these tests were remarkable," he writes. "They revealed the presence of human DNA.

---

24   Ron Tesoriero and Lee Han, *Unseen: The Origin of Life Under the Microscope*, 256.

Strangely though, the scientists were unable to extract a DNA profile."[25] He goes on to say, "There was evidence that the material was human, but no evidence of the combined genetic contribution expected of a mother and a father."[26] He interprets this finding as proof that the sample had no genetic profile *for theological reasons*, opining that since the sample might be from Jesus Christ, it would not have a genetic profile from a biological mother and father since there was no biological father. From there he says that theologians concluded the PCR STR tests were *evidence* that the alleged Eucharistic miracle was telling us that Christ only had maternal DNA.

Given the data, this does not seem like a sound conclusion. Theologically, the exact genetics of Jesus Christ will always remain a mystery.

Various Opinions through the Microscope

The sample was then fixed on a microscope slide and sent to six other scientists for viewing and analysis. Pathologist Robert Lawrence of Delta Pathology Associates in San Francisco was the one who fixed the sample on a microscope slide and viewed it.

He said the sample was epidermis, the external layer of skin, with white blood cells present. His report said there was an "aggregate of keratotic and parakeratotic debris with enmeshed leukocytes." Keratotic growths refer to toughened areas on the skin. Parakeratotic debris refers to flakiness on skin such as in psoriasis and dandruff.

25 Ibid., 48.
26 Ibid., 209.

Additionally, he said there were "scattered minute aggregates of brown material composed of septate hyphal fragments enmeshed in proteinaceous matrix."[27] Hyphae are long tube-like structures that are the basic building blocks of fungi. Fungal hyphae can be septate, divided along the filament by walls called septa (think sausage links), or they can be non-septate with no divisions along the filament (think drinking straws).[28] Matrix proteins are large molecules that tangle into an extensive network of insoluble fibers.

In an interview, Dr. Lawrence said the sample contained white blood cells that were "active living white cells at the time they were collected." He said there was an "inflammatory process going on" and emphasized that "if this material had been placed directly into water after it had been taken off a body, I would expect these cells to be dissolved in minutes to an hour or two."[29] This is, again, a remarkable result! But it is not consistent with the forensic analysis.

Then the slides were sent to Australia for Dr. Peter Ellis, a forensic lecturer at Sydney University, and Dr. Thomas Loy, a molecular archeologist lecturing at Queensland University, both agreeing with Dr. Lawrence that the material was skin.[30] Dr. John Walker of Sydney University thought the material looked like muscle tissue. The sample was also sent to Professor Odoardo Linoli in Italy, the doctor who analyzed the Lanciano Host and blood in the 1970s, and he

27　Ibid., 49.
28　"Septate vs. Non-Septate Hyphae," Biology Dictionary, https://biologydictionary.net/septate-vs-non-septate-hyphae/.
29　Ron Tesoriero and Lee Han, *Unseen: The Origin of Life Under the Microscope*, 49.
30　"In Memoriam, Thomas Harold Loy, 1942 to 2005," http://www.garethloy.com/TomLoy/In_Memoriam_Tom_Loy.html.

concurred that the sample was not only muscle but cardiac muscle tissue.

Ron Tesoriero, the lawyer, documentary producer, and notary who was certifying the investigation and chain of custody for the samples after the investigation began in 1999, explained the different opinions of the scientists who thought the material was skin and the others who thought it was muscle.[31] Healthy heart tissue shows elongated, smooth, striated cells. However, when subjected to trauma, the cells disintegrate and curl, as is documented in pathology atlases. White blood cells infiltrate. Hence he opines that what looked like a scab and fungus could also be damaged, living heart tissue. In September of 2003, Tesoriero took the sample back to Dr. Lawrence, and he confirmed in the light of the other investigations from the scientists that the sample could indeed correspond to tissue of an "inflamed heart."[32] It seems odd that no laboratory tests were done at this point to confirm the presence of white blood cells.

Finally, Ron Tesoriero and Mike Willesee took the microscope slide to Dr. Frederick Zugibe in New York. Zugibe was the chief medical examiner of Rockland County, New York from 1969 to 2002, over three decades in which he performed more than ten thousand autopsies.[33] He held a Bachelor of Science, Master of Science in anatomy and electron microscopy, a PhD in anatomy and

31 Ron Tesoriero and Lee Han, *Unseen: The Origin of Life Under the Microscope*, 49.
32 Institute of St. Clement I, *The Eucharistic Miracles of the World*, p. 6.
33 "Frederick T. Zugibe, M.D., PH.D.," Crucifixion and Shroud Studies: Medical Aspects of the Crucifixion, http://www.crucifixion-shroud .com/bio.htm.

histochemistry, and an MD degree. He was a diplomate of the American Board of Pathology in Anatomic Pathology and Forensic Pathology and a diplomate of the American Board of Family Practice. Dr. Zugibe was an adjunct associate professor of pathology at Columbia University College of Physicians and Surgeons and is a fellow of the College of American Pathologists, a fellow of the American Academy of the Forensic Sciences, Forensic Pathology Section, and a member of the National Association of Medical Examiners.

Zugibe was one of the United States' most prominent forensics experts, known for his work in forensic medicine and for his crucifixion and Shroud of Turin studies.

Dr. Zugibe published a definitive, widely used textbook in a specialized field of diagnostic pathology called *Diagnostic Histochemistry* that is used throughout the world. He has published numerous papers and book chapters in the fields of forensic and general pathology and authored *The Cross and The Shroud, A Medical Examiner Investigates the Crucifixion* (Angelus Books, 1982, 1988) and *The Cross and the Shroud, A Medical Inquiry into the Crucifixion* (Paragon House, 1988). Dr. Zugibe was consulted for his expertise by attorneys and medical examiners from throughout the United States. His expertise was the human heart.

He viewed the microscope slide in April of 2004 and issued a report in March of 2005. Recall that this was five years after the Forensic Analytical genetic report and nine years since the alleged miracle was first observed in Buenos Aires.

In the report, Dr. Zugibe notes that he had not been given any information to the history of the material. He rendered the following opinion, and it is indeed stunning.

> The slide consists of cardiac (heart) tissue that displays degenerative changes of the myocardial tissue (cardiac muscular tissue) with loss of striations, nuclear pyknosis, aggregates of mixed Inflammatory cells consisting of aggregates of chronic inflammatory cells (macrophages) which are the predominant cells admixed with smaller numbers of acute inflammatory cells (white blood cells) primarily polymorphonuclear leukocytes. The directionality of the myocardial fibers indicates that the site of these changes is relatively close to a valvular region in the ventricular area of the heart.
>
> These degenerative changes are consistent with a recent myocardial infarction of a few days duration due to an obstruction of a coronary artery that supplies nutriments and oxygen to an area of heart muscle. The above type changes suggests that the individual had a heart attack a few days prior to death due to obstruction of a coronary artery due to atheroscerosis (a process of fatty plaque buildup in the coronary artery), or due to a coronary thrombosis (clot formation within a coronary artery) the latter either caused by the atherosclerosis process or to injury to the chest wall causing injury to the coronary arteries that supply oxygen and nutriments to the heart muscle). The dating of the injury is derived from the finding a predominance of chronic inflammatory cells, degenerative changes of the myocardium with loss of striations, pyknosis of the nuclei, etc.
>
> When I was later told that the heart tissue was kept in tap water for about a month and transferred to sterile, distilled water for three years, I indicated that it would be impossible to see white blood cells or macrophages in the sample. Moreover, it would be impossible to identify the tissue, *per se* as there would be no morphological characteristics.[34]

---

34   Ron Tesoriero and Lee Han, *Unseen: The Origin of Life Under the Microscope*, 248. Note: the text is exactly as given in the report

Dr. Zugibe's analysis went further than any other scientist. To summarize, the sample looked to him like heart muscle from a person who suffered a heart injury and only recently died at the time of the microscope slide preparation. The white blood cells and macrophages are evidence of injury, as are the obstructed arteries. As he was viewing the microscope slide for the first time, Dr. Zugibe explained in the video that the tissue looked like it came from the left ventricle. This would be remarkable because it is the part of the heart that pumps the oxygenated blood out to the rest of the body.

Also during the video, Dr. Zugibe opined that the patient's heart sample indicated he had been unable to breathe at certain moments because oxygen could not reach him, that he "labored and suffered much because every breath was painful." Zugibe also said that the patient probably received a blow to the chest.

Even more stunning, Zugibe said that the "heart showed dynamic (life) activity" at the moment the sample was brought to him in New York. He explained that this was because he saw intact white blood cells. Since white blood cells are transported by blood and because they decompose quickly after removal from the body, Zugibe concluded "at the moment you brought me the sample, it was pulsating."[35] Afterwards, Zugibe was told the sample came from a consecrated Host that was almost a decade old, and greatly moved, he exclaimed, "I do not believe it." He also

---

printed in the book.

35   Institute of St. Clement I, *The Eucharistic Miracles of the World*, p. 6.

declared, "At the moment you brought me this sample, the heart was alive!"[36]

From this information, Tesoriero and Willesee relayed that a theologian explained the findings as symbolic, that "the Lord in this miracle wanted to show us His myocardium, which is the muscle that gives life to the whole heart, just as the Eucharist does with the Church."[37]

Scientific Scrutiny

These findings invoke deep emotion in the mind of the believer. They also demand an objective consideration free of bias, which can be very difficult, especially in matters that deal with Eucharistic miracles. If this case were on trial in a court of law, and this set of evidence were presented, jurors and a judge would have the task of determining whether there is enough evidence to support a judgment as true. The evidence comes down to whether the testimonies of the witnesses and the doctors who viewed the microscope slides are true, especially since the most awesome conclusions were not supported by laboratory analysis.

There are other questions too. We do not know for sure whether the Host found in the candle holder was consecrated or not. The assumption is that it was since unconsecrated Hosts are kept in the sacristy and only consecrated Hosts are given to parishioners during the distribution of Holy Communion.

What if the Host was not from the August 15, 1996 evening Mass but had been there for a long time? This would

---

36   Ibid., p. 7.
37   Ibid., p. 7.

not substantially alter the strength of the claims, but the Host was very dirty. No one knows for sure how much dust and environmental contaminants it was exposed to, including how many times it was touched by other people. There was no documented chain of custody during this time.

And how do we know for sure that no one tampered with it during the eleven days it sat in the open bowl or tap water in the tabernacle? If the investigators knew the significance of a notarized chain of custody after the investigation began, then they are compelled to admit no such guardianship existed during the three years the sample was kept at Santa Maria parish.

How can we possibly know the chemical nature of the red substance that was sent to Forensic Analytical? The solid grew over several weeks in a red liquid in a bowl of tap water and was transferred to a test tube of distilled water. If the priests thought it was indeed miraculous heart tissue, it seems they would have alerted someone to investigate sooner. Why wasn't the red liquid also analyzed? Why did the solid sample sit in the test tube of distilled water for three years before anyone thought to analyze it? What led to the investigation that began in 1999? Why were the scientists chosen to analyze the sample on four different continents when any number of scientists could have examined the materials under a microscope? It seems a truly blind examination would need to be done by scientists who had never been involved with the study of Eucharistic miracles and who did not already know about each other's work.

There are also some peculiarities in the relationships. Ricardo Castañon Gomez told Tesoriero in 1999 that the woman with the stigmata they had previously interviewed in Bolivia had a message from Jesus. In his biography, *Reason to Believe*, Tesoriero said that Castañon Gomez relayed the message from Jesus through the woman, "Tell Ricardo I want him to take charge of this case. Through it I want to bring dignity back to my altars."[38] She told him that Jesus is upset people no longer believe in His Real Presence in the Eucharist and that people have lost respect, that the investigation of this miracle is part of a plan, that Jesus is suffering.

Castañon Gomez then told Tesoriero that the newly ordained Archbishop Bergoglio contacted him and asked the team to investigate. However, as noted earlier, there is no explanation for this, as Bergoglio could have ordered an investigation sooner.

Ron Tesoriero and Mike Willesee produced the documentary series *Signs from God: Science Tests Faith* in 1998 on FOX television. They would have been in the process of furthering the series when the investigation began in 1999. Dr. Zugibe had also published his book on the crucifixion and the Shroud of Turin in the 1980s, so it seems very likely the parties knew each other. How blind was the test when Zugibe looked through the microscope at an unknown sample while being filmed by two known documentary-makers? Wouldn't he have at least suspected they were visiting him and filming his reaction because it was related to an alleged miracle? His report of living myocardium tissue from the left ventricle, which supplies purified blood to the whole body, almost seems to be a case of something being too good to be true.

---

38   Ron Tesoriero, *Reason to Believe: A Personal Story by Ron Tesoriero* (Cincumber, 2007), p. 89.

If such an extraordinary occurrence like living tissue that was, by then, nine years old really existed, why wouldn't more chemical analysis have been done to prove that the white blood cells that defied genetic profiling were truly there? If the sample had lasted that long, there certainly would have been reason to believe it was robust enough for further testing.

It certainly would be reasonable to conclude that this set of forensic evidence would fail to not only hold up in a court of law but also pass the peer review process for scientific publication. Forensic testing presumes the victim is human, and while there are tests to rule out a human source of tissues or fluids, the tests that would go on to positively identify the chemical makeup of a substance would need more precise screening, spectroscopic, imaging, and genomic testing, especially given the extraordinary claims.

Furthermore, a peer-reviewed paper would present more information about the rationale for the methods chosen, and if found incomplete or unconvincing by peers who guard the integrity of the journal, more tests would need to be done. A conclusion in science should always be supported by multiple sets of tests that all point to the same interpretation, or at least specify what would need to be done for better confirmation. The veracity of this alleged miracle comes down to the testimony of investigators and reporters whose choices in how to conduct and interpret the analysis are unexplained.

Tesoriero also uses the forensic analysis to call for a reinterpretation of evolutionary biology. He asserts that the miraculous appearance of blood or muscle tissue from the consecrated Host is evidence that life *spontaneously arises from innate matter*, harkening back to the seventeenth century when natural scientists thought life spontaneously sprang from nonliving material because they saw decaying meat produce maggots, mud produce fish, and grain produce mice. Spontaneous generation was a reasonable explanation for what people observed, but this theory has long been disproven by evolutionary science.

Tesoriero invokes Charles Darwin from *On the Origin of the Species* when he conceded, "If it could be demonstrated that any complex organ existed, which could not possibly have been formed by numerous, successive, slight modifications, my theory would absolutely break down."[39] Tesoriero says definitively, "It is an assertion never made before: Complex life has spontaneously arisen from inert matter in modern times. For the first time ever life has been shown to exist which did not come from other life."[40] He goes on to argue extensively that these findings refute the educated consensus in biology textbooks, which teaches that all life on earth, plant and animal, evolved from inanimate matter, asserting with confidence that evolution has been proven false.

It is important to keep in mind that any of these alleged miracles could absolutely be possible, for God can do anything at any time. The forensic testing, however, is inconclusive, and the microscopic analysis does not seem to have been truly blind. While more testing could be done to further investigate the chemical composition of the samples, recasting all of

---

39 Charles Darwin, *On the Origin of Species by Means of Natural Selection, or the Preservation of Favoured Races in the Struggle for Life* (London: John Murray, 1859), p. 189.

40 Ron Tesoriero and Lee Han, *Unseen: The Origin of Life Under the Microscope*, 86.

evolutionary biology—even if the miracles happened—is still not warranted. This is another unsound conclusion.

In addition to the FOX documentary series, Castañon Gomez became a speaker presenting the data from these investigations. In a talk on Eucharistic miracles delivered at the National Shrine of the Divine Mercy on December 11, 2012, Gomez explained that he gives around three hundred talks per year.[41] He presents the findings in the same way Tesoriero does, with certainty about the truth of the miraculous claims even though the evidence is inconclusive.

Gomez tells the audience that in blind studies, it was confirmed that the sample was human blood with human DNA but that the DNA *defied* genetic profiling. He says that in multiple studies from other investigations, researchers continued to get the same result—that is, no result (NR) in the PCR test. But he does not explain the limitations of the test or why human handling would have interfered with the analysis.

He says that the labs report that they cannot amplify DNA if it is deteriorated or simply not there. Gomez says of the report from the forensic lab, "They don't know that this is the result I need!" In other words, he needed the DNA test to show there was no DNA, which is exactly what it showed, but he does not explain the most likely reason: that perhaps no DNA was present for analysis. Gomez, like Tesoriero, instead explains that if the Father is the Holy

---

41   Ricardo Castañon Gomez, "Eucharistic Miracles with Dr. Castanon at the National Shrine of The Divine Mercy," National Shrine of The Divine Mercy, December 11, 2012, https://www.thedivinemercy.org /audio/eucharistic-miracles-ricardo-castanon-2012-12-11.

Spirit, there would be no genetic profile typical of humans with paternal and maternal contributions.

To complete the story, in February of 2001, Pope John Paul II made Archbishop Bergoglio a cardinal. The 1996 Buenos Aires final report was presented to Cardinal Bergoglio on March 17, 2006, almost ten years after the Host was found in the candle holder.

The newest book on Eucharistic miracles by Dr. Franco Serafini tells how witnesses knew of Cardinal Bergoglio's once per year Eucharistic adoration at Santa Maria parish in Buenos Aires in which he would kneel for an hour in the church where this event occurred.[42] Serafini notes that even after the investigation, this case is only designated a Eucharistic sign in the diocese and was never declared a miracle. Fragments of the Host are exposed on the altar in a chapel at Santa Maria parish, and the Host is treated with discretion.

Perhaps the truth is that there is simply no absolute scientific investigation that would remove all doubt about whether the consecrated Host exuded or became human blood and muscle. But there is enough evidence here to inspire better methods for investigating these reports.

---

42 Franco Serafini, *Un cardiologo visita Gesù. I miracoli eucaristici alla prova della scienza* (Bologna: ESD-Edizioni Studio Domenicano, 2018); Ary Waldir Ramos Diaz, "The future Pope Francis was in charge of dealing with this reported Eucharistic miracle," *Aleteia*, June 13, 2020, https://aleteia.org/2020/06/13/the-future-pope -francis-was-in-charge-of-dealing-with-this-reported-eucharistic -miracle/.

Review/Summary

Key Ideas

- In the 1990s, four Eucharistic miracles were reported in Buenos Aires, Argentina—two in 1992, another in 1994, and another in 1996—all at the same parish of Santa Maria on Avenue la Plata. Only the alleged miracle in 1996 was investigated scientifically.

- The archbishop of Buenos Aires in 1999, who would become Pope Francis, appointed Ricardo Castañon Gomez as the lead scientist, along with Ron Tesoriero, an attorney, and Mike Willesee, a journalist, to record the investigation.

- The report from May of 2000 on the 1996 alleged Eucharistic miracle reported that no blood was detected in the sample and that there may have been some DNA but not enough for successful STR analysis. Per routine forensic analysis, the sample was simply reported as non-biological material with possible DNA contamination and a "NR," for "no results," on the PCR STR test.

- The 1996 sample was fixed on a microscope slide and sent to six other scientists for viewing and analysis. They reported the presence of white blood cells, indicating the tissue was living, but no laboratory tests were done to confirm this finding.

- The plausibility of this alleged miracle comes down to the testimony of investigators and reporters whose choices in how to conduct and interpret the analysis are unexplained.

Good Facts to Memorize

- Christ is present "whole and entire" in every part. In the consecrated Host, He is present whole and entire. Christ is present whole and entire in every fragment. The breaking of the bread does not divide Christ. Therefore, Christ is present whole and entire in a fragment that fell, even by mistake, onto the corporal.
- Nearly 99 percent of all humans' DNA share mostly the same sequences. What makes us each unique at the biological level is the specific combination of DNA sequences we inherit from our parents that code for proteins to produce our physical traits.
- These findings invoke deep emotion in the mind of the believer. They also demand an objective consideration free of bias, which can be very difficult, especially in matters that deal with Eucharistic miracles.

Effective Questions to Ask When
Discussing the Real Presence

- What are the limitations of various scientific analytical methods?
- Why is it important to understand how analytical methods work and assess a sample?
- What should we do if a single test result looks promising?
- When is it appropriate for theological conclusions to be drawn from scientific investigations?
- What are the dangers in too easily representing a scientific result as absolutely true?

THE LANCIANO REPORT

The Historical Timeline

THE oldest report of a Eucharistic miracle dates from AD 750 in Lanciano, Italy. This miracle involved both the bread turning into flesh and the wine turning into blood. The flesh is sealed in glass in a special monstrance, and the blood is coagulated into five pellets. Both species underwent scientific analysis in 1970 and 1971 by Professor Odoardo Linoli, the same professor who was asked much later in the early 2000s to view the microscope slide from the 1996 Buenos Aires sample mentioned in the previous chapter.

In this case, Professor Linoli was the first to declare that the flesh is striated cardiac muscle tissue based on chromatography and immuno-hematography tests. He also identified that both samples were human and contained no preservatives to keep them in their condition from the 700s to the present day. He also reported the blood type as that of AB blood.

A book by Bruno Sammaciccia titled *The Eucharistic Miracle of Lanciano, Italy* (*Il Miracolo di Lanciano*), translated into English from Italian in 1976, offers great insights into the Lanciano miracle. Specifically, this book, with an imprimatur for both translations, provides both the historical timeline of the event and the full Linoli report (as it is called) that was published in a scientific journal. The short book has a bibliography of books, historical documents, and scientific texts consulted.

The people of Lanciano have long held a devotion to their "Miraculous Relics" from the ancient times of the Church.[1] There are annual festivities and solemnities, and the bishops and archbishops join with the mayor to celebrate. The timeline is worth reviewing to gain an appreciation of the efforts to authenticate the event as miraculous.

The historical account begins about eight hundred years after the miracle is said to have happened. In 1536, a bull by Pius IV ordered that "nothing is to be renewed" in the Church of St. Legontian, where the holy relics resided. In 1557, a testament of the account was written by Mastro Ferdinando Di Giovanni del Barbiero and notarized by Giovanni Angelo Di Faxio. Then in 1574, the first authentication was made on a marble tablet that is still on display.

Verified in the presence of a group of people, it is reported that the total weight of the five pellets of congealed blood is equal to the weight of each one of them. This authentication has not ever been repeatable in subsequent authentications.

Later in 1586, Father Tossignano recorded that in the Church of St. Francis of Lanciano, "there is found the host of flesh miraculously changed into the Body of Christ, there are also found Relics of the miraculous Blood." In 1593, the Marchesa di Vasto visited Lanciano, saw the

---

1   Bruno Sammaciccia, *The Eucharistic Miracle of Lanciano, Italy*, trans. Francis J. Kuba (Trumbull: E. J. Kuba, 1976), p. 38.

body and blood, and had them transferred to the cathedral by the Conventual Fathers.[2]

In the late 1500s and 1600s, Ferdinando Ughelli writes of the miracle in the Monastery of St. Francis. He says that there are many relics there but the sacrament of the Most Holy Eucharist, which he notes was changed a thousand years ago into flesh and five pellets of blood, is the greatest relic of all. There are other accounts recorded by admirers.

In 1601, His Excellency the Duke of Monteleone records that he saw the relics. In 1610, there is a report of an ordination in the church where the Most Sacred Body resides. In 1631, Bishop Andrea Gervasio asserted that the Church of St. Francis in Lanciano venerates a miraculous Host changed into the flesh of Christ and coagulated blood. These documents are all referenced in Sammaciccia's book.

In 1637, the holy relics were transferred to the Valsecca Chapel where Friar Serfina Da Scanno, the Father Guardian at the Church of St. Francis, made a second authentication. He declared, "In the year 700, in the abovementioned Monastery at the time called S. Legontian, in which Basilian monks resided, while a certain monk was having doubts concerning faith in the Most Holy Sacrament of the Eucharist, as (he) pronounced the words of the consecration within the Mass, there occurred before the people that great miracle of the bread changed into Flesh and of the wine changed into Blood."[3]

In 1671, Monsignor Alfonso Alvarez Barba Ossorio defined the relics of Lanciano as "the Greatest and Stupendous Relic of Relics." A year later, in 1672, Pope Clement

---

2   Ibid., p. 39.
3   Ibid., p. 40.

X declared the altar of the holy relics a privileged altar on
the octave day of the deceased and on all Mondays of the
year. In 1685, Abbot Giovanni Battista Pacichelli wrote,
"In the ancient Temple of S. Francesco, at one time belonging to the Monks of S. Basil, later the Monks of Cassino,
among many relics, there is preserved with great venera-
tion, the Sacred Host changed into Flesh and some drops
of wine changed into Blood, one thousand years ago at the
hand of an unbelieving Religious Priest, the story of which
is depicted in the Sacristy."[4]

In 1700, Bernardino De Cecco's last will and testament
asked that fifty Masses be celebrated in the Chapel of the
Relics in the Church of San Francesco following his death.
In 1717, Archbishop Giovanni Uva ordered for the key to the
chapel to be given to him, only in 1728 for Monsignor Antonio Paterno to order the keys to remain with Reverend Don
Silvesto De Cecco while the archepiscopal see was vacant.

In 1743, Carol Cinerini, the magistrate of the city of Lanciano, mentioned the relics by name in a decree. In 1787,
Monsignor Archbishop De Vivo records a visit to the Host.
The point here is that there is a continuous record through
time of the most holy relics of Lanciano, even though the
record started eight hundred years after the incident is said
to have occurred. This historical record is important, however, because it shows that these, the most holy relics of
Lanciano, were really there.

In 1799, Archbishop Francesco Amoroso granted the citizens permission to hold a procession of penance using the
relics, and in 1800, the Duke of Monteyasi, Chamberlain
of His Majesty the King, by Royal Order of the House of

_____
4   Ibid., p. 41.

Naples inquired about the sanctuary of special devotion. In 1868, a procession was held due to forty-five days of rain that flooded the countryside, and it is said that during the procession from the chapel to the square, the wind broke up the storm clouds.

In 1866, Cardinal Gaetano Alimonda wrote to Reverend Sanna Solaro that he was sending a priest to Lanciano for certification of the miracle before a commission of ecclesiastics. In 1889, Reverend Solaro, president of the Italian Society of Eucharistic Displays, produced a banner inscribed, "Compliment of the Archbishop, Clergy and People of Lanciano," to be taken to France. And in 1904, Monsignor Angelo Dalla Cioppa established the Association of Daily Adoration at the altar of the holy relics.

The scientific investigation conducted by Dr. Odoardo Linoli was not commenced until November 18, 1970 at 10:00 a.m. in the sacristy of the Church of St. Francis before the entire community of the monastery.[5] Dr. Linoli was a professor at large of anatomy and pathological histology and of chemistry and clinical microscopy, and he was the head physician of the United Hospitals of Arezzo.

At 10:15 that morning, His Excellency Monsignor Pacifico Perantoni, archbishop of Lanciano and bishop of Ortona broke the seals on the chalice and the monstrance, and the knowledge of modern science was brought to bear on the twelve-hundred-year-old relics.

---

5   Ibid., p. 44.

The 1970 Scientific Analysis

The essential experiments and finding from Dr. Linoli's lab will be first reviewed as they were presented on March 4, 1971. These findings were published under the title "Histological, Immunological and Biochemical Research of the Flesh and Blood of the Eucharistic Miracle of Lanciano," in *Quaderni Sclavo di Diagnostica*, Siena in 1971. It is important to consider his work in full before discussing it fifty years later in the context of more modern methods.

Commencement of the Investigation

Upon opening the moon-shaped container made of glass, it was discovered that the relics were in an unsealed container. Mold and other substances were observed under a microscope. Dr. Linoli expressed concern that a laboratory analysis would be inconclusive because he thought the flesh would not have any identifiable substance in it.[6]

The pellets of blood were weighed upon removal from the sealed chalice. The total weight of all five was determined and the individual weights were measured but not recorded. This statement was given in the authentication that day: "The phenomenon of the identical weight of one pellet as against the other four, attested to by Mons. Rodriquez in the authentication made by him on February 17, 1574 and recorded on a marble tablet of 1636 located on the side of the altar of the Miracle in the Church of St. Francis was not verified, just as it had not been verified in the authentication of 1886."[7]

---

6   Ibid., p. 44.
7   Ibid., p. 44.

Appearance of the Samples

Dr. Linoli used great precision and effort to record the appearance of the flesh and blood. The tissue was described as irregularly roundish in form with a void in the center, such that the tissue seems drawn to the edges like that of a rind. The tissue facing the center was frayed and small bits protruded into the center void. The color was yellow-brown-chestnut with browner spots and streaks and white specks.[8] He also noted tiny perforations on the rim of the tissue that were evenly spaced as if they were sewn in the past.

Linoli was given permission to touch the flesh sample. He reported that it felt uniformly hard like wood. The white specs were easily detached without clinging to the rest of the sample. Linoli also noted residuals of small dead insects and larvae.

The white specs were tested for starch using iodo-iodide solution and viewed under a microscope. The results were negative for starch. Starch is a carbohydrate. If the sample were bread, it would have tested positive. It was also noted that "conspicuous accumulations of spores and of hypha of hyphomycetes" were present in all microscope observations. These looked like microscopic fungi, which would constitute the whitish specks adhering to the sample.[9]

In the chalice, the pellets were described as solid formations with superimposed irregularities on one another, suggesting the substance may have coagulated and divided. The surface was finely wrinkled with curves running downward. The color was yellow chestnut. The fragments had the appearance of chalk, coarse, also with white specks. The

8   Ibid., p. 47.
9   Ibid., p. 49.

substance was hard and left a dust in the bottom of the chalice. The white specks, unlike on the tissue, were part of the substance and therefore said not to be parasitic or extraneous in nature. The weight of the five fragments was 15.85 grams in total.

Fragments of both the tissue and the pellets were taken: 20 mg of the flesh from the edge of the tissue and 318 mg from a blood pellet.[10]

Histological Study of the Flesh and the Blood

The 20 mg fragment of tissue was used to investigate the sample under a microscope. First the tissue was rehydrated and fixed to the slide through successively increased concentrations of alcohol. Then, per usual, the sample was placed in paraffin, sliced thinly with a microtome, and stained as a sample of muscle tissue and connective tissue would be stained.

The report says that the nuclei of ancient tissues do not stain due to a homogenization of the cells.[11] Here the report says that the histological observations "led to assurance of absolute objectivity."[12] Dr. Linoli said he was sure the tissue was not an epithelial lining but of mesodermal derivation. The cells in tissues on the external areas look different than cells of internal tissues.

He also noted that the tissue was not collagenous or leio-muscular (smooth). He opined that the tissue was fibrous muscular tissue based on morphological characteristics.[13]

10   Ibid., p. 50.
11   Ibid., p. 53.
12   Ibid.
13   Ibid.

The specimen showed fibers of varying thickness. He also noted that the fibers connected end to end, ribbon-like, connecting so that the tissue is a complex mass of connected fibers. He said, "These results lead, no other view being deemed possible, to the recognition of a striated muscular tissue of the myocardium."[14] There was also fatty tissue visible, proper to cardiac muscle. Linoli also did not see any other substance impregnating the tissue as would be expected if chemical preservatives were present.

He concluded that the nature of the tissue was muscular and striated, the fibers were connected end to end by ribbon-like distensions and by the coupling and continuity of one fiber with another, the fibers were in varied directions, and the fibers penetrated into a lobe of adipose fatty tissue. The flesh, he said, "consists of striated muscular tissue of the myocardium."[15]

The results were affirmed by Ruggero Bertelli, professor emeritus of normal human anatomy of the University of Siena. Though altered by time, the two experts concurred on the identity of the samples.

The microscopic study of the blood pellet also began with rehydration, fixation, clarification, microtome sectioning in paraffin, and staining. No cells were observed. Instead, a net-like filamentary substance was present with lumpy nodules of varying size. A granular substance was also present that was suspected to derive from hemoglobin.

---

14   Ibid., p. 54.
15   Ibid., p. 55.

Chemical Test on the Blood

Per the usual methods, the tiny part of the pellet was dissolved on a glass slide and subjected to reagents that detect
the hemoglobin, hydrochloride hematine, and hemochro-
mogen. These were run alongside a control sample of
human blood. The tests were negative, indicating that time,
exposure to light, and oxidation in the air caused hemoglobin, a pigment, to decompose. A negative test for hemoglobin does not, therefore, lead to the conclusion that the
sample is not blood.

As described in the Buenos Aires investigation, the
ortho-tolidine test detects the oxidation of glucose. This test
was positive for glucose, which is noteworthy but again not
definitive since it is a presumptive test rather than a confirmatory test.[16] Other substances can produce a positive test
as well, such as vegetable extracts or finely ground metals.

Thin-Layer Chromatography of the Blood

Thin-layer chromatography (TLC) is another technique
that compares a substance to a control. It works by separat-
ing different components of a mixture based on the relative
attractions of each component to a substrate. For TLC, the
thin layer of absorbent material used was silica gel.

Multiple samples can be tested at the same time on the
same strip with a low potential for cross-contamination
between samples. The solutions are placed on a baseline
and allowed to develop for a set time. Then the movement

---

16   Ibid., pp. 55–58.

of the different components along the silica gel are measured against controls.

Dr. Linoli prepared two solutions of normal blood (oxyhemoglobin and alkaline hematine) and a third solution from the blood pellet. These three samples were run simultaneously three times to provide a result. On a sheet of silica gel that was 20 cm by 20 cm, three sets of the three solutions rose along the silica all to the same height. Linoli reported that the controls and the test sample all had the "perfect alignment of the stains which have the same Rf (=0.88)."[17]

The Rf is a measurement of the degree of retention of a component in TLC called the retardation factor. It does not have units since both lower and upper values are distance traveled; it is calculated as the distance traveled by the component divided by the distance traveled by the solvent the component is dissolved in.

Linoli concluded that the chromatographic experiment demonstrates "with absolute certainty that the solid matter, defined as the Blood of the Miracle of Lanciano, is truly blood and this ascertainment constitutes a definitive and indisputable response for the purpose of the problem presented."[18] In other words, he was absolutely certain the chromatographic analysis proved the miracle.

17 Ibid., pp. 58–59.
18 Ibid., p. 59.

Immunological Studies to Determine Species (Human)

Having shown that the samples are myocardial muscle tissue and blood, the next test determined if the specimens were human. To do this, the zonal precipitation reaction of Uhlenhuth was used.

This test is best known for its use in blood typing. It was developed in 1901 by a German scientist named Paul Uhlenhuth for the investigation of a double murder.[19] It is also used to distinguish human from non-human blood because antigens in a sample will coagulate with the test serum containing antibodies. Samples are placed in test tubes with the precipitating serum. The analysis is read by whether a precipitate forms. Test Tube 1 contained the blood, 2 the flesh. Test tubes 3 through 7 contained positive human blood controls and negative animal (rabbit, bovine serum) controls.[20] The test for both the blood and the flesh were positive for human.

Dr. Linoli reported that the reaction of Uhlenhuth demonstrates "in an absolutely clear manner the immunological encounter that was established between the commercial precipitating non-human serum and the antigens still present in the Blood (test tube #1) and the Flesh (test tube #2)."[21] The tests were repeated on two different days. He determined that both samples were human blood and human flesh.

---

19   "Uhlenhuth Test," American Forensics, http://www.americanforensics.org/uhlenhuth-test/.

20   Bruno Sammaciccia, *The Eucharistic Miracle of Lanciano, Italy*, pp. 60–61.

21   Ibid., p. 62.

Blood Type Determination

Since the tissues were old, Linoli used a method that does not rely on the presence of red blood cells to determine the blood type, opting instead for one that relies on the presence of antibodies. To do this, he immersed strips of blotting paper in the solutions of flesh and blood and fixed them in methanol. The strips were then exposed to two serums, agglutinate serum anti A and agglutinate serum anti B.[22] Controls were also prepared in the same way. The test strips were refrigerated overnight so the antibodies in the serums could bind with any antigens in the samples and controls. The strips were then heated to dissociate the antibodies and antigens, freeing the antibodies into a new solution.

The liquid with the detached antibodies was transferred to test tubes. Human blood of known type A and type B was added to the respective test tubes. If the blood and flesh had any type A or type B antigens present, they would bind to antibodies in the serums. Then the type-specific antibodies would be released in the new solution, and the antigens on the known type A and type B human blood would bind to those antibodies in solution, forming an agglomerate. This is the typical method for typing blood.

The blood and the flesh both reacted with both type A and type B antibodies. The controls did not form agglomerates.

Linoli concluded that the "delicate immune hematological proof of the absorption elution permits us to assert with complete objectivity and certainty that the Blood and the

---

22   Ibid., pp. 63–64.

Flesh of the Eucharistic Miracle of Lanciano belong to the same blood type AB."[23]

Linoli also noted that just because the blood types are the same for each sample, does not necessarily mean the flesh and blood are from the same person. It could belong to two different people with the same blood type.

Electrophoresis of Proteins

Dr. Linoli tested for the proteins in the samples. This test determines the percentage of the components of albumin and globulins in the tissue. In humans, albumin is a protein made in the liver that keeps fluids in the bloodstream from leaking into other tissues. It carries substances throughout the body.[24] Globulins are bigger proteins made in both the liver and immune system.

Electrophoresis is like chromatography in that solutions of the samples and controls are placed in a substrate and separated according to chemical properties. In this test, the substrate is cellular acetate, and the movement is caused by an electric field that moves charged particles. (Electrophoresis means to move electrons.) Large molecules will separate according to size and binding affinity due to charges on the surface of the proteins.

The test results are given by the equipment in a diagram called an electrophoretogram. The components are deposited on the substrate as they move in the electric field, and the peaks on the diagram show the relative quantities of

---

23   Ibid., p. 65.
24   "Albumin Blood Test," Medline Plus, https://medlineplus.gov/lab
     -tests/albumin-blood-test/.

each component. The serum protein electrophoresis diagram for human blood has a distinct form. The peak for albumin is large since it is the main protein in human blood plasma (the liquid component of blood). The globulins, which are bigger molecules, deposit later, but their peaks are smaller since there is less of them in the serum.

Dr. Linoli ran controls along with the samples from the blood only and was surprised ("it is truly wondrous") that proteins obtained from such an ancient sample had the profile of fresh serum in which the percentages of proteins are in the normal distribution.[25] He concluded that the electrophoretic graph "proves to be of fully normal type and contributes so much more to define the profile of the true Blood of the Eucharistic Miracle of Lanciano."[26]

Determination of Blood Salts

Finally, Dr. Linoli researched the mineral components in the blood. He pulverized a 100 mg dried fragment of the blood in a mortar and transferred it to a test tube with distilled water. The powder floated in the water. For controls, he used blood specimens from normal subjects of varying ages, dried the blood in a desiccator for several weeks, and prepared them the same way. He also prepared a control serum with salts in the percentages expected in normal human blood.

Using a variety of simple analytical methods, he precipitated the chlorides and phosphorous. To determine the

25 Bruno Sammaciccia, *The Eucharistic Miracle of Lanciano, Italy*, pp. 66–67.
26 Ibid., p. 67.

level of calcium and magnesium, he used a spectrophotometer for atomic absorption. All elements have characteristic absorption spectra caused by their electron configurations. Potassium and sodium were determined by flame photometry. Then the blood sample was compared with the controls.

The results showed that the blood contained chlorides, phosphorous, magnesium, potassium, and sodium. The relative percentages were different for the desiccated samples of human blood from various aged people compared to the control serum for fresh blood. Desiccation results in the loss of phosphorous, chlorides, and potassium but not magnesium and sodium.

The blood sample had a distribution of salts comparable to the desiccates samples of fresh human blood, except sodium, which was low but still within normal limits. Linoli reported that "the components of the Blood of Lanciano stood up throughout the centuries in a manner not unlike that of the desiccated control-blood."[27]

He did note that the calcium content was greatly increased, however. This can be accounted for because the sample was stored in glass for centuries. It is known that ions of salts can exchange between substances in contact, which is why it is well-known in the field of chemistry that plastic containers should be used to store some solutions rather than glass. In addition, the presence of dust could have skewed the calcium result.

27   Ibid., p. 68.

Conclusion from the Linoli Report

Because the famous Linoli report findings are the most salient feature, they frequently overshadow the complex research involved. The previous discussion of the methods is intended to provide a record of the care that went into the analysis in 1970. Conclusions should be considered in the context of the methods. Having reviewed the methods, here are the closing statements from Professor Linoli:[28]

1. The blood of the Eucharistic miracle is real blood, and the flesh is real flesh.
2. The flesh consists of the muscular tissue of the heart.
3. The blood and the flesh belong to the same human species.
4. The blood type is identical in the blood and in the flesh, and this stands to indicate that the donor is a single person, whilst there remains open the possibility of their origin from two different persons who, however, have the same blood type.
5. In the blood, there were found normally fractioned proteins with the percentual proportions that are found in the sero-protein scope of normal fresh blood.
6. In the blood, it was discovered that the minerals chlorides, phosphorous, magnesium, potassium, and sodium were present in a reduced quantity, whereas calcium was found in an increased quantity.

---

28   Ibid., p. 70.

He then addressed the diagnosis of myocardium tissue in the flesh, a diagnosis he admits is left to the expert interpretation while viewing through a microscope. Dr. Linoli suggested that the way the sample was cut disproved any possible fraud perpetrated centuries ago. He stated that "only a hand experienced in anatomic dissection would have been able to obtain from a hollow organ such a uniform cut (as can still be glimpsed in the Flesh) and cut tangentially at that to the surface of the organ, as suggested by the prevalently longitudinal course of the fascicles of muscular fibers, in many instance visible in histological preparations."[29]

In other words, Dr. Linoli is saying that the Host-sized round cut was made inside the heart, as opposed to the outside surface. He contended that the cut went from the inner surface and then around into the muscle. This is a significant observation. Usually, tissue is cut using a die to remove a circle of tissue on the inner lining.

Finally, Dr. Linoli noted that if the blood had been taken from a cadaver, it would have been more decayed and altered. He emphasized that the blood had the composition of fresh but desiccated blood and contained no abnormal salt concentrations indicative of the preservatives used in mummification.

Commentary

What follows now is the author's commentary on the Linoli report. Each section will be taken in the same order as it was presented in the original report. Additionally, there are

---

29   Ibid., pp. 70–71.

extra commentaries as appropriate. This approach seemed the best way to analyze what we know today about the Eucharistic miracle of Lanciano.

Commentary on the Commencement of the Investigation

The *great reverence* given to the Eucharistic miracle of Lanciano was seen in the formal investigation, which commenced on November 18, 1970 before the monastic community and was presented in the Chapel of St. Francis on March 4, 1971, almost four months later.

The scientific investigation was not presented as a proof of faith, and this is the most important aspect of this investigation to bear in mind as the data is critiqued. Linoli's report was, instead, considered a third authentication that followed the one in 1574 on a marble tablet and the second in 1637 when the relics were transferred. It is perhaps a subtlety, but a point of great importance that underscores the meaning of Dr. Linoli's work. *The relics had been accepted as the flesh and blood of the miracle of Lanciano for centuries.* Hence, this scientific examination was enacted to gain more knowledge of the physical substances. Or in the profound words of Dr. Linoli stated here:

> May precious attention and profound respect be given to these proofs which science has offered us, not only in the moral sense, not only for the principle of believing and accepting, but above all honestly and seriously for the love of the truth, and reality.
>
> Do not approach the reading of the technical, biological, and analytical data exposed in the following pages, as you would a common blood analysis or as a mere cultural

fact, medical, chemical and histological: but read with that devotion and with that intimate acceptance which will be the fulfillment of whatever every reader will find in himself, in order better to understand and better to have a feeling for the lofty but not rhetorical significance of the result of this recent authentication.

For the first time in the course of history, at least inasmuch as the Eucharistic Miracle of Lanciano is concerned, science, equipped with exceptional and precise means, offers us categorical data which confirm the validity and the certainty about the Eucharistic Miracle treated above; now all that remains is to accept and meditate.[30]

Everyone involved already accepted this miracle as being true. The entire report shows that Dr. Linoli approached the study of not just possible flesh and possible blood, but *the* flesh and the blood of the miracle of Lanciano.

Recall that he even noted in the beginning of the investigation that he expressed fear of not being able to reach any scientific conclusions. He took great effort to record his process in detail, knowing better methods would come along in later years. Further, he explained his decisions and conclusions, which surely aided in the findings being published in a scientific journal, *Quaderni Sclavo di Diagnostica*.

This journal is likely tied to the Sclavo Diagnostics International company in Italy, founded by Achille Sclavo. In 1904, Sclavo developed the serum against anthrax, and in 1929, the Sclavo Institute began producing other vaccines for diphtheria, tetanus, and smallpox. In 1934, the company began making diagnostic products.

The historical record shows that reverence was long given to the miracle, so it is reasonable to assume that a

---

30   Bruno Sammaciccia, *The Eucharistic Miracle of Lanciano, Italy* (*Il Miracolo di Lanciano*) (Trumbull: Rev. Francis J. Kuba, 1976), p. 50.

detailed scientific study would not have been disparaged by an Italian scientific company and journal but perhaps greatly appreciated and encouraged. If more studies of alleged miracles were approached with the same rigor and caution, perhaps they would be published in scientific journals as well.

Commentary on the Existence of a World Health Organization Study

In the Catalogue of the Vatican International Exhibition titled *The Eucharistic Miracles of the World*, there is a well-known story about how the Lanciano report aroused great interest in the scientific world, so much so that in 1973, the chief advisory board of the World Health Organization (WHO) appointed a scientific commission to conduct their own investigation of Dr. Linoli's work. The book says:

> Their work lasted 15 months and included 500 tests. It was verified that the fragments taken from Lanciano could in no way be likened to mummified tissue. As to the nature of the fragment of flesh, the commission declared it to be living tissue because it responded rapidly to all the clinical reactions distinctive of living beings. The Flesh and the Blood of Lanciano are just that, flesh and blood, in the same condition one would expect to find flesh and blood taken the same day from a living human. Their reply fully corroborated Professor Linoli's conclusions. The extract summarizing the scientific work of the Medical Commission of the WHO and the UN, published in Dec. 1976 in New York and Geneva, declared that science, aware of its limits, has come to a halt, face to face with the impossibility of giving an explanation.[31]

31   The Real Presence Eucharistic Education and Adoration Association, Inc., *Catalogue of the Vatican International Exhibition: The Eucharistic Miracles of the World* (Bardstown: Eternal Life, 2016), 133.

Anyone who reads that statement wants to verify it, and with the internet, the task should be simple. However, one would search in vain for such a report, as well as for the medical commission or declaration on two continents. The content of the claim is even exaggerated.

Finally, in 2018, a medical doctor, Dr. Franco Serafini, published a book in Italy. He visited many sites where Eucharistic miracles were reported and investigated the claims. He traveled to Lanciano and found the WHO report in a safe upon requesting to see it. He scheduled a whole afternoon to study it but said that after a couple of minutes, it was clear that the WHO declaration was a "terrible fraud, a terrible hoax, very sad."[32]

There were hundreds of pages of tests, but the tests were on Egyptian mummies, not the Lanciano miracle. A first and last page had been added mentioning the work of Dr. Linoli, but that was all. The origin of the story of the WHO report is still unknown, but it is evidence that some people were willing to go to lengths to begin and propagate false information to trick the faithful into believing something that was not true. Eucharistic miracles are not matters of faith in Christ but of faith in people, a distinction that cannot be stressed enough.

Commentary on the Appearance of the Samples

Dr. Linoli noted the details of the appearances, and they certainly seemed to be old. It is worth repeating that the

---

32   "Interview on Eucharistic Miracles with Cardiologist and Author, Dr. Franco Serafini," *The Joy of Faith* (podcast), September 4, 2020, https://youtu.be/51_dFa-K8lI, 9:00; Franco Serafini, *Un cardiologo visita Gesù. I miracoli eucaristici alla prova della scienza* (Bologna: ESD-Edizioni Studio Domenicano, 2018).

surprising account of the weights of the pellets of blood was not authenticated in 1637 or in 1970. The weight of the five pellets total did not equal the weight of each one. The weights of all five were also not identical.

Oddly, however, Dr. Linoli did not record the individual weights. Supposedly, it was sufficient to note the total was not the same as the individuals, but this oversight seems inconsistent with the otherwise keen attention to detail.

Nevertheless, the story is still told today as it was in 1574, and this is a cause for concern. Most notably, this account is misrepresented in the recent book *Catalogue of the Vatican International Exhibition: The Eucharistic Miracles of the World*, presented by the Real Presence Eucharistic Education and Adoration Association (2016). The stories, over one hundred in number and spanning twenty countries, are authored by the young Blessed Carlo Acutis, who died at the age of fifteen of leukemia.

Blessed Carlo Acutis's devotion to the Eucharist was great, and he traveled around the world to see the Eucharistic miracles and write about them in his short life. The miracle of Lanciano is, of course, the oldest account, and of the pellets of blood, the book says, "In the Blood of the miracle can be recognized all the components present in fresh blood, and the miracle within the miracle: each of the 5 clots of Blood weighs 15.85 grams, which is the identical weight of the 5 clots weighted together!"[33]

The excitement is admirable, but since the book is titled as a catalogue of the "Vatican International Exhibition," it

33 The Real Presence Eucharistic Education and Adoration Association, Inc., *Catalogue of the Vatican International Exhibition: The Eucharistic Miracles of the World*, 134.

seems to carry the weight of Church approval. It would be reasonable for a reader to assume this claim is true without researching the history of the Lanciano account to discover this was not the case even back to 1637.

The reason to be careful is that small misrepresentations can cast doubt on the retelling of the entire account of any miracle, which is why humility is essential, especially imitating Dr. Linoli's humility when assessing historical and scientific presentations.

Commentary on the Histological Study of the Flesh and the Blood

After the naked eye, a microscope is the most straightforward way to observe samples. Here we must rely on images selected by Dr. Linoli to tell the story. Indeed, one places faith in scientists who view, photograph, and interpret microscope slides. We do not know what the rest of the material looked like, but we can assume that photographs were selected to present the best possible visualization.

This is expected, but without scanning the sample yourself, it is impossible to appreciate the pervasiveness of the appearance. Still, because Dr. Linoli is an expert in these matters, it is reasonable to trust his observation. Note, this analysis can only prove what the tissues appeared to be, and the samples were admittedly altered by time, dehydrated in storage for centuries, rehydrated in the lab, fixed in alcohol, embedded in paraffin, sliced, and stained. They looked like striated myocardial tissue, and it adds to the confidence of this conclusion that another professor concurred.

Commentary on the
Chemical and TLC Tests on the Blood

These tests are good reminders of how to interpret chemical tests. Without knowing the exact atomic composition and structure of all the compounds, including impurities that are always present in samples in the natural state, it is not possible to chemically define a substance absolutely. In chemistry, a substance is defined by the chemical composition. Substances are known to react with each other in certain ways, but when they do not react as expected, as was the case for the negative result for the hemoglobin test, the result does not necessarily mean that the substance is not what you think it is.

As Dr. Linoli explained earlier, the lack of chemical response for hemoglobin could mean that the hemoglobin once present had decomposed. The sample could have been blood in which the hemoglobin oxidized, a reasonable explanation for an ancient sample. The positive result for the glucose test does not define that the sample was blood. As Dr. Linoli noted, other substances can react with the reagents similarly. A chemist strives to understand observations and make comparisons.

Likewise, for the TLC results, the sample taken from the chalice patterned the solutions of normal blood in this particular test. This is a reliable indicator that the test sample is the same as the controls because the speed with which a chemical moves along a strip of absorbent material is a function of its composition, all other things being equal.

Commentary on the
Immunological and Blood Type Studies

Those familiar with Eucharistic miracles know that the AB blood type occurs in every report, including those from the Shroud of Turin studies. In fact, AB is believed to be the most common type in men from the region where Jesus Christ lived. Understandably, this claim excites many people, for it sounds like Christ is peeking through relics to show Himself to us across time and space. It would be tempting to conclude that all these relics come from the same man.

However, a search for truth also demands a consideration about the limitations of these tests. Dr. Kelly P. Kearse, an immunologist, former principal investigator at the National Institute of Health, and author of a textbook in the methods of molecular biology, has provided an opinion on the blood type studies. He is agnostic on the veracity of the miraculous blood types.[34]

Blood tests are presumptive tests in that they evaluate the possibility that blood may be present.[35] Blood tests detect hemoglobin, the molecule in red blood cells responsible for carrying oxygen to the body. Hemoglobin is also a pigment and leaves the red stains. Fresh blood is straightforward to

---

34 "Shroud of Turin's Bloodstains: An Interview with Blood Expert Dr. Kelly Kearse," Real Seeker Ministries, https://anchor.fm/real-seeker -ministries/episodes/Shroud-of-Turins-Bloodstains-An-Interview -with-Blood-Expert-Dr--Kelly-Kearse-eav4on.

35 Kelly Kearse, "A Critical (Re)evaluation of the Shroud of Turin Blood Data: Strength of Evidence in the Characterization of the Bloodstains," Shroud of Turin website, https://www.shroud.com/ pdfs/stlkearsepaper.pdf.

measure, but aged samples are more difficult. Hemoglobin oxidizes easily, so it is a straightforward detection. If there is hemoglobin, there is probably blood. But as we saw, if there is no hemoglobin, possibly because the sample is old, there could still be blood, but another test would be needed.

The chemical tests detect oxidase activity in the hemoglobin, but in an old sample with unknown history, other molecules can also react similarly, giving false positives. Or the samples can give false negatives if the coagulated specimen does not dissolve in the solution.[36] So, to say blood cannot be detected is not to say that blood is not or never was present.

Blood consists of red blood cells that contain the hemoglobin and white blood cells. In addition to the cells, blood also is made of a liquid serum. When hemoglobin is not found, other components in the serum can be tested for, notably albumin, which as was noted in the electrophoresis, comprises most of the serum protein. Immunoglobulins are also present as part of the immune system. There are five classes denoted (IgM, IgG, IgD, IgA, IgE). Determining if the blood is human is more difficult.[37] Recall that in the immunological studies, antibodies triggered against human proteins, thus making them specific to human proteins. This type of test, however, cannot determine whether blood from another species could also be present.

In the case of the Shroud, this might be more important. Howeber, in the Eucharistic miracle of Lanciano, it is doubtful the blood belongs to, say, a rabbit or pig, but it could, and the test would not detect it. Genetically close species would

---

36 Ibid.
37 Ibid.

respond to a human-specific antibody, so as far as what species of blood there was, according to Kearse, "the best, most scientifically objective conclusion is that primate blood has been detected."[38] More conservatively, it is correct to state that primate blood components are present.

That statement may seem overly scrutinizing, but this concept matters in the ABO typing as well, or even more so. ABO refers to molecules called antigens (antibody generators) on the surface of red blood cells. Blood typing measures the presence or absence of antibodies in the serum.

In a case where the person is known, the blood type test is straightforward. Our blood cells have about two million ABO molecules on each surface. Type A individuals have A molecules on their red blood cells, and type B have B molecules.[39] Type O individuals have neither A nor B. These molecules are carbohydrate (sugar) molecules with a core (same) structure and chemical differences on the ends for A or B; type O only have the core structure.

In what is called "forward typing," the sample is tested and gives, in these cases, a positive result for type AB, meaning there were antibodies produced for the A and B antigen molecules. Dr. Linoli also ran controls without the blood sample, and they were negative for type AB. This much testing is done on the Eucharistic miracles that report type AB blood.

However, there is a possibility in old samples for a false positive. The ABO antigens are not unique to humans.[40] These molecules are also found in other species, such as

38   Ibid.
39   Ibid.
40   Ibid.

bacteria, fungi, and insects, which Dr. Linoli reported present visually in the samples.

A better verification could be done, according to Dr. Kearse, who reminds us of the way blood transfusions are done. If a patient is getting a blood transfusion, the medical professionals need to be certain the blood will not coagulate and cause the patient to die. "Reverse typing" is also done to complement the forward test. Humans also have antibodies in their serum against the molecules *they do not have on their red blood cells.*

Type A people have anti-B antibodies. This is because when a foreign type B molecule is encountered in a type A person's blood, the immune system naturally produces antibodies to bind it and protect the person. (This is how the body also protects itself against viruses.) So a reverse typing would look for anti-B antibodies in a person who tested positive for type A. This applies for type B individuals as well. A person who is type O will have antibodies against both A and B. In the case of the blood for the miracle of Lanciano, a type AB serum would have neither anti-A nor anti-B antibodies present because both A and B molecules are already present on the red blood cells.

In blood transfusions, the complementary tests ensure that wrong blood is not used since antigens and their specific antibodies bind and coagulate. With blood samples that have aged, the antibodies can degrade over time, so even if a reverse typing is done, the antibodies that were once there may not be detectable.[41]

---

41   Kelly P. Kearse, "The Relics of Jesus and Eucharistic Miracles: The Significance of Type AB blood," Academia.

To put all that together in the context of the Lanciano blood sample and any other Eucharistic miracle blood report, if there were a situation in which bacteria, fungi, or insects caused a type AB forward typing, and the reverse typing were not done, or could not be done, the test would be inconclusive.

The sample could be type AB blood, but the blood test is not necessarily proof that the sample is indisputably type AB blood. Further, even if a reverse test were done, there is no way to determine if that result is due to the absence of antibodies or the degradation of antibodies that were once there. Unfortunately, the ABO blood typing tests for Eucharistic miracles are all inconclusive for this reason.

Commentary on the
Electrophoresis of Proteins

Electrophoresis measurements are semi-quantitative. Since the tests separate charged large molecules from small molecules in an electric field, the test does not give a positive identification of the chemical composition of the components separated. If they are run against controls, as Dr. Linoli did with human blood, the most that be concluded is that the sample could be the same as the control, although it is undeniably remarkable that the controls and tests were so close a match.

Just as in the blood typing test, electrophoresis is a first-round test that would need to be followed with more tests to know whether there were other large molecules that deposited the same way the control molecules did. The test results indicate that there are large molecules, the size of albumin, in the sample. Genetic testing or mass spectroscopy could provide more information. Dr. Linoli used the tools of his time, but today, a "truly wonderous" result would warrant further testing.

Commentary on the
Determination of Blood Salts

These results, again, confirm the presence of salts, but this is not a surprising finding. Like the other tests, these results are inconclusive in determining the identity of the sample, although they are useful data points to add to further testing if it is ever done in the future.

Commentary on the
Conclusions of the Linoli Report

Professor Linoli's findings are repeated throughout the world in books, blog posts, academic articles, and talks. There is no doubt that Dr. Linoli showed the greatest reverence for the Eucharistic miracle of Lanciano, and that is his greatest legacy. His scientific testing was done in service to the truth and his love for Christ and the Church. He performed his duties with humility and honor. Because scientists search for truth, or at least they ought, they know that all results are always subject to improvement.

The conclusions can, therefore, be amended for modern times:

1. The blood of the Eucharistic miracle has characteristics of desiccated human blood, but due to

aging and unknown amounts of contamination,
the immunological, chromatographic, and electrophoresis tests are inconclusive.

2. The flesh appears to consist of the muscular tis-
    sue of the heart as viewed under a microscope.
3. The blood and the flesh test positive for a pri-
    mate species.
4. The blood type showed identical forward testing
    results in the blood and in the flesh for type AB,
    but these tests are inconclusive. Reverse testing
    of the serum antibodies was not done.
5. In the blood, there were found normally frac-
    tioned proteins with the percentual proportions
    that are found in the sero-protein scope of desic-
    cated normal fresh blood.
6. In the blood, there were also discovered the
    minerals chlorides, phosphorous, magnesium,
    potassium, and sodium in a reduced quantity,
    whereas calcium was found in an increased
    quantity.

Regarding the way the sample was cut, it does not necessarily follow that a hand experienced in anatomic dissection could only have made the Host-shaped specimen, as
Linoli suggested. The opinion is valuable, but again, it is
simply not conclusive.

None of the scientific investigations can prove that
bread turned into flesh. They only analyze the substance at
hand. Data is only as good as its weakest link, so without
a verifiable eyewitness and chain of custody, the scientific
tests remain inconclusive on the question of a physical and

chemical substance change. It comes down to what testimony we choose to believe.

None of the samples are dated with radiometric methods, so in a cold, hard technical sense, science cannot say anything about preservation.

If the sample turned to flesh in 700, and if the sample is the same one that was in the monstrance all those centuries, and if it was never tampered with, and if any natural explanation (desiccation) could be ruled out, then it would be remarkable that the protein profile gives the result it does. Additional tests could be done, but there will always be unanswered questions. Ultimately, it will come down to what testimony we choose to believe—and we can unquestionably believe that Christ physically changed the bread and wine into His biological flesh and blood. But we cannot rely on science to explain these profound mysteries, but instead, we must believe with the eyes of faith.

Review/Summary

Key Ideas

- The Eucharistic miracle of Lanciano has a long historical record dating back to the 1500s, and it has been honored there for centuries.
- This Eucharistic miracle had the first extensive scientific testing, published in a scientific journal in Italy by Professor Odoardo Linoli in the 1970s.
- The 1970 Linoli report was a very detailed and cautious study. Today, in the context of more modern methods, its results are inconclusive as to the identity of the samples.

Good Facts to Memorize

- The historical account of the Eucharistic miracle of Lanciano begins about eight hundred years after the miracle is said to have happened.
- In 1574, the first authentication was made on a marble tablet that is still on display. Verified in the presence of a group of people, it was reported that the total weight of the five pellets of congealed blood were equal to the weight of each one of them. This authentication has not ever been repeatable in subsequent authentications.
- In 1637, the holy relics were transferred to the Valsecca Chapel where a second authentication was made.
- The scientific investigation conducted by Dr. Odoardo Linoli commenced on November 18, 1970

at 10:00 a.m. in the sacristy of the Church of St. Francis before the entire monastic community.

- The tests done by Dr. Linoli were weighing, histological studies, chemical tests, thin-layer chromatography, immunological studies to determine species and ABO blood type, electro-phoresis of proteins, and presence of blood salts.

Effective Questions to Ask When Discussing the Real Presence

- How would the identity of the miraculous blood and flesh be confirmed using modern scientific methods?
- Why are the tests said to be inconclusive?
- How can we talk about these miracles in a reverent way?
- Does it really matter to faith if science ever proves or disproves the case of this (or any other) miracle?

CONCLUSION

DON'T PUT YOUR FAITH ON TRIAL

"You shall not put the Lord, your God, to the test."
—Matthew 4:7

EVEN if the most sophisticated genetic tests of modern times were employed, no scientific investigation could ever prove that Christ is truly present in the Holy Eucharist. This will always be a matter of faith. Without biological samples from Christ's body to ascertain His DNA when He walked the earth, we do not have material for a comparison. We could, at most, prove that a physical change takes place, and for that proof to be as certain as possible, a group of people who witnessed a change would need to meticulously report the details.

If these individuals were scientifically inclined, then all the better. Perhaps the ideal scenario would involve a group of scientists and doctors attending the same Mass when a consecrated Host turned into flesh and blood so that an investigation could commence immediately. Perhaps samples would be collected with reverence and in the manner most appropriate for analytical methods. Then using the most modern scientific methods, a full chemical and genetic analysis could be conducted to not only know the DNA makeup but also to know the exact composition of tissue and blood. The samples would be stored correctly, the data analyzed by including yet more groups of dedicated scientists and doctors who had no reason to be biased about the outcome, the results debated, more tests ordered, more discussion allowed, until the day the final report is given with a level of consensus. Even if such a scenario were to happen, some level of debate would continue as the science moves forward.

We do not have those samples, though. The most we could hope for is an exact DNA match each time the miracles happened. Additionally, there is an inherent problem in the investigations because there are no good controls for testing. To assess the samples that have been stored for years, decades, or centuries, the best scientific analysis would involve a Host that did not bleed or become tissue but that sat next to the one that did, exposed to the same environmental changes and subjected to the same natural decomposition. This is one aspect that separates analysis of Eucharistic miracles from the analysis of the Shroud of Turin. On the cloth, there are abundant such controls in the sections that are not suspected of containing blood.

Perhaps for future Eucharistic miracles there could be a protocol for a congregation or celebrant to follow if someone sees a Host bleed or become tissue or the wine becomes physiological blood. At that point, the Vatican should convene a team of scientists and doctors to write a plan detailing how to collect and store the sample, where to send the samples for the same testing each time, who to include in the analysis, and how to report the results compared to a bank of data.

Of utmost importance in any investigation, however, is that there be no fabricated information to play on the tenderness of people's hearts and minds, only a straightforward, transparent scientific assessment. All involved in these investigations have an obligation to protect against dishonesty and exaggeration. Frauds and hoaxes are horrible betrayals. Such behaviors violate every virtue, both cardinal and theological. To misrepresent the Real Presence of Christ in the Eucharist either to bring fame or fortune upon oneself is to betray all sense of authentic faith in Christ.

If a miracle is reported, the people investigating it have a responsibility to the Body of Christ, which is the Church, and to all the people of the world who might be inspired to deeper faith. Great care and tentative language should be used to avoid any exaggeration, which means rigorous and humble scientific analysis is necessary, following the example of Dr. Linoli.

Even those who wish to make videos or retell the accounts of Eucharistic miracles in books and presentations have an obligation to avoid the sloth of uncritical repetition. We should not simply retell what we hear but rather adopt a healthy spirit of critical thinking. Question claims. Seek answers. Offer better solutions. As the Bolsena and the Lanciano miracles reveal, the Catholic Church has a rich tradition that has been passed down, and these reports have been treated mostly with great reverence. But as we also saw with each of the three miracles reviewed, we must also be on the lookout for incomplete information. Caution is not the same as stubborn skepticism, where we refuse to believe what we cannot observe ourselves.

Likewise, numerous pieces of evidence point, though not conclusively, to the Real Presence in the Eucharist throughout the centuries and through multiple human and scientific accounts. As difficult as it is to *conclusively* prove a scientific fact even with the most meticulous research related to these miracles, it would be equally difficult to conclusively disprove several pieces of the data as well, such as the testimony of the scientist who looked through microscopes.

The scientific evidence for Eucharistic miracles is like numerous seeds being planted. As we experience all that is good, true, and beautiful in life, so the "scientific evidence" for the Eucharist miracles can be like seeds that affirm our faith more than irrefutable proofs to convince the doubter. The mind of the Creator of science and reason will always be beyond our reach. The real miracle is that He sent His Son to make us His children, revealed to ourselves who we are, and saved us from death.[1]

And if you find yourself afraid to accept that what you have heard about the Eucharistic miracles may not be true, if you find that your faith *depends* on these miracles, please pause and dig deep. Why do you need the miracles to be true? Do you doubt? If so, pray for clarity and courage to address your uncertainty or disbelief, for you are not alone. Even St. Thomas had doubts until Christ appeared with His wounds so Thomas could touch them. Ask God for the gift of theological faith, and it will be granted to you. Christ will come to you too.

---

1   I am grateful to Dr. Oscar Paniagua, the father of the girl whom this book is dedicated to, for sharing these concluding insights. They are mostly his words.

So, dear reader, do not put your faith on trial with the science of the Eucharistic miracles, because scientific knowledge is *always, always* incomplete. At some point, too much faith in the science and testimony of Eucharistic miracles becomes impious. It is to succumb to the scientism and materialism of our day, and even Christians must guard against an overreliance on the senses. It is useful to recall the warning given in the Catechism of the Council of Trent in 1563. "Pastors, aware of the warning of the Apostle that those who discern not the body of the Lord are guilty of a most grave crime, should first of all impress on the minds of the faithful the necessity of detaching, as much as possible, their mind and understanding from the dominion of the senses; for if they believe that this Sacrament contains only what the senses disclose, they will of necessity fall into enormous impiety."[2]

Having exhausted scientific analysis of any Eucharistic miracle, pushing the best analytical methods of our time to the limits, knowledge will never provide the certainty we seek. We will ultimately rely on faith.

Hebrews 11:1 tells us, "Faith is the realization of what is hoped for and evidence of things not seen." *Faith is the evidence of things unseen.* Ultimately, when we stop trying to see with our biological eyes, we will see with our spiritual eyes. We do not believe that Christ is truly present in the Holy Eucharist, that the bread and wine become the body and blood of Christ, because of any physical miracle.

We believe this greatest of miracles because Christ said so.

---

2 Council of Trent, "The Sacrament of the Eucharist," Catholic Apologetics Information, http://catholicapologetics.info/thechurch/catechism/Holy7Sacraments-Eucharist.shtml.

We believe what Christ said, and indeed everything Christ said, because in the purest and simplest way possible, we believe in Christ. The order in the universe is evidence of a Creator. "Because of it the ancients well attested. It was not by knowledge that the human race knew the universe was ordered by the word of God, so that what is visible came into being through the invisible" (Heb 11:2–3). All of Hebrews 11 is a journey through faith. Faith precedes miracles! By faith, Enoch was taken up. By faith, Noah warned about what was not yet seen. By faith, Abraham obeyed so that there came forth from one man "descendants as numerous as the stars in the sky and as countless as the sands on the seashore." By faith, Moses kept the Passover. By faith, women received back their dead through resurrection. And by faith, we live today.

Christ really walked among us. Christ really died for our sins, rose from the dead, and ascended into heaven. The sacraments are real. Christ is really present in the Holy Eucharist, and we can be with Him, personally and physically, in every Mass where we taste and see with the eyes of faith. And when we receive His body, blood, soul, and divinity in the Sacred Host with the burning faith of the saints like Ignatius of Antioch, Justin Martyr, Irenaeus of Lyons, and Cyril of Jerusalem, we can be assured that He says to us, "Behold, it is I."

"Look at my hands and my feet, that it is I myself. Touch me and see, because a ghost does not have flesh and bones as you can see I have."

—Luke 24:39

BIBLIOGRAPHY

Augustine. *Contra Faustum*. http://www.newadvent.org/
fathers/140626.htm.

Catalogue of the Vatican International Exhibition: The Eucharistic Miracles of the World, Presented by the Real Presence Eucharistic Education and Adoration Association, Inc. Bardstown: Eternal Life, 2016.

Catholic Encyclopedia, The. New York: Robert Appleton Company, 1911.

Cruz, Joan Carroll. *Eucharistic Miracles and the Eucharistic Phenomena in the Lives of the Saints*. Charlotte: TAN Books, 1987.

Darwin, Charles. *On the Origin of Species by Means of Natural Selection, or the Preservation of Favoured Races in the Struggle for Life*. London: John Murray, 1859.

Diaz, Ary Waldir Ramos. "The future Pope Francis was in charge of dealing with this reported Eucharistic miracle." *Aleteia*. June 6, 2020. https://aleteia.org/2020/06/13/the-future-pope
-francis-was-in-charge-of-dealing-with this-reported
-eucharistic-miracle/.

Denzinger, Heinrich. *Compendium of Creeds, Definitions, and Declarations on Matters of Faith and Morals*. Edited by Peter Hünermann. 43rd ed. San Francisco, CA: Ignatius Press, 2013.

Donaldson, James and Alexander Roberts. *Ante-Nicene Christian Library: Translations of the Writings of the Fathers Down to A. D. 325*. Edinburgh: T. and T. Clark.

Geng, Tao and Richard Mathies. "Minimizing inhibition of PCR-STR typing using digital agarose droplet microfluidics." *Forensic Science International: Genetics*. Volume 14 (January 2015).

Holmes, Michael W. *The Apostolic Fathers in English*. Grand Rapids, MI: Baker Academic, 2006.

Institute of St. Clement I. *The Eucharistic Miracles of the World (I Miracoli Eucaristici nel mondo. Catalogo della mostra internazionale.)*. Bardstown, KY: Eternal Life, 2016.

Kearse, Kelly. "A Critical (Re)evaluation of the Shroud of Turin Blood Data: Strength of Evidence in the Characterization of the Bloodstains." Shroud of Turin website. https://www.shroud.com/pdfs/stlkearsepaper.pdf.

Ott, Ludwig. *Fundamentals of Catholic Dogma*. Charlotte: TAN Books, 1974.

Palmer, Douglas. "Flow cytometric determination of residual white blood cell levels in preserved samples from leukoreduced blood products." *Transfusion*. Vol. 48 (January 2008).

Real Presence Eucharistic Education and Adoration Association, Inc., The, *Catalogue of the Vatican International Exhibition: The Eucharistic Miracles of the World*. Bardstown: Eternal Life, 2016.

Roberts, Alexander, James Donaldson, and A. Cleveland Coxe, eds. *Ante-Nicene Fathers*, Vol. 1. Translated by Alexander Roberts and William Rambaut. Buffalo, NY: Christian Literature Publishing Co., 1885.

Rubin, Miri. *Corpus Christi: The Eucharist in Late Medieval Culture*. 1st Edition. Cambridge: Cambridge University Press, 1991.

Sammaciccia, Bruno. *The Eucharistic Miracle of Lanciano, Italy.* Translated by Francis J. Kuba. Trumbull: E. J. Kuba, 1976.

Serafini, Franco. *Un cardiologo visita Gesù. I miracoli eucaristici alla prova della scienza.* Bologna: ESD-Edizioni Studio Domenicano, 2018.

Saiki, Randall et al. "Enzymatic Amplification of β -Globin Genomic Sequences and Restriction Site Analysis for Diagnosis of Sickle Cell Anemia." *Science.* Volume 230, Issue 4732 (December 1985).

Schaff, Philip and Henry Wace, eds. *Nicene and Post-Nicene Fathers, Second Series*, Vol. 7. Translated by Edwin Hamilton Gifford. Buffalo, NY: Christian Literature Publishing Co., 1894.

Schochetman, Gerald et al. "Polymerase Chain Reaction." *The Journal of Infectious Diseases.* Volume 158, Issue 6 (December 1988).

Tesoriero,Ron. *Reason to Believe: A Personal Story by Ron Tesoriero.* Cincumber, 2007.

Tesoriero, Ron and Lee Han. *Unseen: The Origin of Life Under the Microscope.* Kincumber: Tesoriero, 2013.

Turchiano, Michael et al. "Impact of Blood Sample Collection and Processing Methods on Glucose Levels in Community Outreach Studies." *Journal of Environmental and Public Health* (January 2013). https://doi.org/10.1155/2013/256151.

Van Ausdall, Kristen. "Art and Eucharist in the Late Middle Ages." In *A Companion to the Eucharist in the Middle Ages.* Edited by Ian Levy, Gary Macy, Kristen Van Ausdall. Leiden, Boston: Brill, 2012.

Weisheipl, James A. *Friar Thomas D'Aquino: His Life, Thought, and Work.* Garden City: Doubleday, 1974.

DATE DUE

264.02 TRA
234.163

Behold It Is I

St. Stephen the Martyr Catholic Church
13055 SE 192nd St,
Renton, WA 98058